Are You Thinking What I'm Thinking?

A Patchwork Journey Through My Life... So Far

Kenneth Radley

**Are You Thinking What I'm Thinking?
A Patchwork Journey Through My Life… So Far**

About the Author

Kenneth Radley is an iconic Australian actor, and now an author.

He has four grown children and is currently dividing his time between Thailand and Australia

Kenneth Radley

This book is a work of nonfiction and is based on the author's personal memories, experiences, and interpretations. While every effort has been made to ensure accuracy, some names, locations, and identifying details have been changed to protect the privacy of individuals.

The views and opinions expressed are those of the author and do not necessarily reflect the views of any individuals or organisations mentioned.

The author does not intend to defame, malign, or harm any individual, group, company, or entity. Any resemblance to real persons, living or dead, beyond those clearly identified, is purely coincidental.

Events have been recounted to the best of the author's recollection. As memory is subjective, other parties may recall events differently.

Copyright © 2025

**Are You Thinking What I'm Thinking?
A Patchwork Journey Through My Life… So Far**

Dedication

I dedicate this work to my children

Georgia Radley

Angus Radley

Marvin Radley Bell

Angelica Bell Radley

the joy of my life, with love x

Kenneth Radley

Table of Contents

About the Author ii

Dedication iv

Entree 1

The First ABC Open Day In Paramatta, 1994. 5

The Old Man And The Sea 6

What's Going On Over There? 9

Music 12

The Blues 13

Short Cut Road 15

    Sneak Preview 18

    John Farnham 20

    Cold Chisel 21

    The thrill of performance 23

    Jazz 25

    The Power of The Dog 26

    The arrival of the script, the welcome pack, production info 28

    Isotunes 30

    Driving. Four wheels and a full tank 31

    I've been called an 'overthinker'… let me ponder that 33

    Sidney Myer Music Bowl, Melbourne. 1995 34

    Cars 34

    Holden 1964 EH wagon 36

    Vespa 125cc (1959) 37

Are You Thinking What I'm Thinking?
A Patchwork Journey Through My Life... So Far

My first memory and some more… 38

Evidence based behavioural Psych exploration can be fun! 40

Closing ceremony of the Olympic Games, Sydney 2000............ 44

Art can sneak up on us... 45

Cut to 35 years hence… 47

Yamaha 360cc enduro... 49

Bill Hunter 49

Reservoir, a high board, Miss Vagg, Research and… Where actually is my sister? 56

Flashback to Reservoir pool High Diving board… Summer, circa 1964. 62

1969 Bushfires.. 64

VW Superbug 1600… and a call from Sydney. 67

Flying to various cities with Nicholas for the open days. 68

John Jarratt & Fields of Fire 69

The Kombi 71

The Kombi era 73

Cut to late afternoon Winter, Woolamai Beach, Phillip Island..... 74

A lifesaving moment….. 74

The Diesel... 76

Judy Davis & The Detailed Work Of An Expert 78

The Night the Angels Came… 80

The Coffee Shop... 84

Honda 100cc Street Bike and Bruce... 86

Priscilla… and a gently flowing river of experience 89

Kenneth Radley

Martin Sacks	90
The cinematographer is your friend (or should be…)	95
Leadership	96
A Little More on Leadership… Janet	97
Terence Stamp Misses The Target… Or Does He?	104
WAR! What did you do it for?	110
The Last Goodbye	115
The Legacy Of My Father	117
Yamaha XT 250cc (1985) road/trail bike	119
Footy	121
Ten Love!... for Gerard Kennedy	130
True stories from the cabs… (all my stories are true…)	135
Are You Vacant?... and a Chance for a Man to Reflect	139
A Change of Direction	142
Cellarmasters… the wine period	142
Farewell Sydney After 15 Years	146
The Kiss	148
Dirt Blocks and Bridge Timbers	157
Aboriginal History: A Lingering Blight	159
David Gulpilil	166
Bush Beat. Live Music Explodes Into My Life	178
The Susan Street Incident	179
The Art of the Stunt Fight	183
Holden Captiva 2007	186
The Oils. Melbourne Cup Day – sometime in the 90s	187

**Are You Thinking What I'm Thinking?
A Patchwork Journey Through My Life… So Far**

Johnny Depp 189

Mitsubishi Triton Twin Cab. 192

Trumper Oval 193

Unsettling Encounters and the Call to 000 196

VW Golf Gti 2006 198

When the starlight foundation came to the studio 199

The Atrium 200

Bananas; some of the journey 204

A few more Banana notable moments: 211

Michael 211

The final hurrah… 211

The Russian Mafia and the Bananas 212

A small educational segue… 215

Anyways… back to Bananas… 216

B2 finally loses his shit! 217

A Random Gallery… 219

Outro 227

Acknowledgements 228

Are You Thinking What I'm Thinking? A Patchwork Journey Through My Life… So Far

Entree

I tuned in to a wonderful conversation between Julia Louis-Dreyfus and Jane Fonda in the opening episode of Julia's terrific podcast series, Wiser Than Me. It was a fascinating exchange. As I drove steadily through the central west of Victoria, I found myself completely engrossed. The conversation was wide-ranging, loose, delightfully charming and informative full of tantalising tales, belly laughs, and "oh really?" moments.

At one point, Jane spoke about life unfolding in three acts, like plays, films, or classic storytelling. It's a simple structure:

Act 1: 0–30 years

Act 2: 30–60 years

Act 3: 60 to death

A therapist had once suggested that Jane write an account of her life when she hit the "freak-out" age of 59. Not necessarily for anyone else, but primarily to help her focus her thoughts and reflect on the journey so far. The idea was that doing so might influence how she navigates the third act. The process, she said, would certainly stir things up, clarify some events, muddy others, expose a myriad of large and small topics worth reflecting on. A chance to compartmentalise, to laugh, to wonder, to ruminate.

That little moment planted the seed for this: an autobiography, a memoir, a patchwork of reflections. It might just be me going blah! a tendency for which I already have something of a reputation. The style is a little free-range and roundabout. This looseness is welcome in my world, and it's something I actively encourage in my students. I consider it a vital part of critical thinking, helping to foster a flexible approach to learning. Of course, curriculum and content matter. But flexible thinking, and a broad, questioning approach to life and learning, matter more. They fuel understanding, and more importantly, they nurture curiosity.

Are You Thinking What I'm Thinking?
A Patchwork Journey Through My Life… So Far

If I were in charge, digression would be a subject in itself or at the very least, a solid unit of work in secondary schools. We'd go here, which would lead us over there, and then over to somewhere else entirely… and finally I'd ask, How, I wonder, does all this even remotely connect with our original learning intention? Ask students that, and they'll often come back with the most thoughtful and surprising insights.

I love asking students questions. It puts them at ease once they realise I don't, for a second, believe I have all the answers. Because I don't. And frankly, we should be wary of anyone who claims they do. Certainty is dangerous. It starts world wars.

There are no guarantees, just like in life, that my stories and recollections are even accurate. Eyewitness accounts, after all, are among the most unreliable forms of evidence in any courtroom. Here's some anecdotal evidence. (Ha!)

I have a good friend a scientist, sharp as a tack, who always claimed to have an exceptional memory. One day, she had to go to the police station to give a statement about a dramatic event that had happened nearby. Cops were involved, complaints were made. She had no emotional or personal stake in the matter; she just happened to be present. She witnessed everything and, with her supposedly excellent recall, felt certain she could accurately describe who was there, the sequence of events, where people stood, what was said, who got physical, and when.

What she didn't know though, was that there were two CCTV cameras that had captured the entire incident. The police played her the footage. She told me that watching it was deeply humbling: several major details she'd been utterly sure of were completely wrong. The scientist with the razor-sharp, analytical mind had failed the memory test even in this calm, detached scenario.

Proof enough, if you ask me, that memory is unreliable. Science says so.

Are You Thinking What I'm Thinking? A Patchwork Journey Through My Life… So Far

This journey will flip and flop between bananas and building, between thoughts, reflections, and connections with fellow thespians, between action and repose… because that's how life works. You can plan all you like, but shit happens anyway.

So here it is: a patchwork, a roundabout, a strut, a shadow, a moment in time.

And what does it all mean?

Macbeth, 500 years ago, pondered some of these same things upon hearing of his wife's death.

And he still ponders today…

She should have died hereafter;

There would have been a time for such a word.

To-morrow, and to-morrow, and to-morrow,

Creeps in this petty pace from day to day

To the last syllable of recorded time,

And all our yesterdays have lighted fools.

The way to dusty death. Out, out, brief candle!

Life's but a walking shadow, a poor player.

That struts and frets his hour upon the stage.

And then is heard no more: it is a tale Told by an idiot, full of sound and fury, Signifying nothing.

Oscar Wilde said, 'the truth is as malleable as an imperfect memory.'…

(sshhh…) He may or may not have actually said that…

I heard it somewhere and I like it.

I have no evidence.

Kenneth

Are You Thinking What I'm Thinking?
A Patchwork Journey Through My Life... So Far

In the car… thinking… possibly about to make a decision

Are You Thinking What I'm Thinking? A Patchwork Journey Through My Life… So Far

The First ABC Open Day In Paramatta, 1994.

Marquees, ABC celebrities, presenters, and stars were everywhere giving demonstrations, engaging with the public, and soaking up the buzz. What a brilliant idea: the national broadcaster is truly for the people. A 25,000-strong crowd gathered in front of the main stage, chanting, "Bananas! Bananas!" The moment we bounced onto the stage to perform our 15-minute pre-recorded mini-show, the place erupted.

Following the strong video sales, sky-high ratings, and the complete sell-out of all available merchandise, this Taylor Swift-level response to our live appearance felt like the ultimate confirmation: the Bananas were taking off in a seriously big way.

Over the following years, the Bananas headlined several ABC open days in capital cities across the country. Each event was packed with energy, laughter, and excitement. It was always a highlight, and always enormous fun.

B1 asking 25,000 of his closest friends if they've seen his support star?

Are You Thinking What I'm Thinking?
A Patchwork Journey Through My Life... So Far

The Old Man And The Sea

This was one of the finest moments of my teaching life and indeed, my life.

Some time ago, I came across a short excerpt from *The Old Man and the Sea*, the Pulitzer Prize-winning novella by the great Ernest Hemingway, regarded by many as his best work. I had never read it myself, though I had once portrayed a character named Elziver Block in a promenade theatre production of *Moonfleet*, who was loosely based on Hemingway's old man.

At the time, I was doing some teaching at a secondary college in Melbourne. On this particular morning, stirred by that brief encounter with Hemingway's writing, I asked Ryan, a terrific young assistant in the library if we had a copy of *The Old Man and the Sea*. Without hesitation, he strode over, picked it off the shelf, and handed it to me.

I thanked him and took it to my Year 7 literacy class. These students are bursting with sparks, promise, ideas, and a sensitivity that can brighten your day. (And yes, they can be a little challenging at times.)

I'm a storyteller. I tell my students this. I also tell them that storytellers make better surgeons, better police officers, better bus drivers, better prime ministers. Stories are vital in our lives. Students *hear* the story. Teachers! Stop trying to cram them full of content. Use stories. The content and meaning will follow. It always does.

So, I told my restless Year 7s: "Each lesson, after your usual ten minutes of silent reading your novel, or your muscle car magazine, or whatever you've brought, I'll read two paragraphs from this renowned novella." And so I did.

I'm a good reader. There's no need for false modesty. I know how to pace the words, wrap my mouth around them, bring the characters to life. I know when to whip through it, when to slow down. I'm an actor of some experience. This is what we do.

Are You Thinking What I'm Thinking? A Patchwork Journey Through My Life… So Far

Over the following weeks, they began to connect with the story, the style, the nuance, the quiet power at its core. They felt the relationship between the boy, the old man, the fish, and the sea. They didn't always understand the nautical terms or equipment; the tiller, the bow, the wind directions or the ancient baseball references. Joe DiMaggio? "Who's that?" they'd ask. It didn't matter. "He's a legend," I'd say, and they'd get it.

And as the story unfolded, they began to ask for it. They told me they loved hearing it.

"Mr Radley, we love the way you read this story."

That kind of comment means the world, especially coming from kids.

Then came the last lesson of Term 3 *today*. Twelve pages left.

I spoke firmly to the fidgety boys, "You want me to read? Then you need to be still." And to their credit, they were. The only girl in the group, a delightful human who loves horses, watched me and the pages with quiet intensity.

I read on. Hemingway guided us gently but powerfully through those final pages. The emotional weight, the craftsmanship. No bloody wonder it won a Pulitzer. A couple of times, I had to pause, quietly, to hold myself together. I'm easily moved, but I didn't want them to see that. My job was to read.

The ending was perfect. Of course it was.

And when I finished, I paused. Then, this: my students, spontaneously, applauded. I'm not joking. In a small room in a Melbourne college, six lively Year 7 students were moved to offer genuine strong applause because they had been *touched* by truly great writing.

It was a profound moment.

I told them, quietly, that I thought they might never forget it. I know I won't.

Are You Thinking What I'm Thinking?
A Patchwork Journey Through My Life… So Far

In the final ten minutes of class, I asked them to write briefly about their favourite part of the story, to imagine what might have happened next, and then to draw something inspired by the book: the boat, the sea, the characters or the great marlin the old man had come to know so well. Eighteen feet long, 5.4 metres, we stepped it out on the floor. Enormous.

One of the students, borrowing a pen from me, drew a picture. "Can I have a boomerang, sir?" I call them boomerangs because they need to come back. He struggles with words and spelling, and with unravelling the tricky meanings behind text. But oh my God when I saw his quick sketch of the fish, discreet tears welled up again.

Stories. Oh, how we need stories.

He stayed back after class. Looked me in the eye. "Thank you for teaching us, sir," he said, and shook my hand.

"Thank you, mate. Good luck to you," I replied, and watched as he slowly sauntered off to recess.

It doesn't get better than this.

The sketch, a boy's response to brilliant storytelling

Are You Thinking What I'm Thinking? A Patchwork Journey Through My Life... So Far

What's Going On Over There?

In the winter of 1973, I had just turned fifteen.

At dusk, I was outside our home on Valley Road in Research, Victoria, Australia, when I noticed some noise and bright lights about 200 metres away, near the corner of Ingrams Road and Main Road, just by the Research shops. Not much happened in Research in those days, so I wandered over to check it out.

There were lights, cars, people, caravans, small trucks, and loud conversations. Radios were clicking on and off. I found a spot to settle in and quietly observed the scene. I was watching the setup for a television shoot. Mesmerised, I worked up the courage to ask one of the crew what show or film they were working on. "*Matlock*," came the reply.

Matlock Police was a highly successful series made by Crawford Productions, with around 250 episodes produced over several years. It starred Michael Pate, a crusty Australian actor who had enjoyed some success in Hollywood as the head detective. Grigor Taylor, a handsome NIDA graduate, played the stern young detective, and Paul Cronin portrayed the likeable motorcycle cop from the fictional country town of Matlock. And here they were preparing to shoot, just across the road from my house!

I stayed and stayed, trying to make sense of what I was seeing. My brother Peter eventually came over to tell me Mum had served dinner and I was needed at home. No way. This was big. This was *something*. I stayed, and didn't return home until after midnight, when I scraped together something to eat.

The episode, I later discovered, was titled *Daniel*. It followed the story of a young man recently released from gaol who returned to Matlock just as a series of attacks on young women began to plague the town. He was a troubled soul, and quickly became the prime suspect.

Are You Thinking What I'm Thinking?
A Patchwork Journey Through My Life... So Far

Daniel was played by Chris Haywood a fabulous actor who would go on to become a solid and iconic presence in Australian cinema. Over the decades, he has graced our screens with a wide range of acclaimed performances, and is held in deep respect within the industry. I didn't meet Chris that night. I only remember him sitting alone in a director's chair on the edge of Ingrams Road smoking, playing with a dog, leaning forward, head bowed. Then someone called him to set. Time to shoot the scene.

In that moment, Daniel grabbed a girl and carried her down the road in a rough, undignified manner, his hand covering her mouth. It was intense and dramatic. The crew seemed satisfied with the take. Chris disappeared into the makeup van and then into a production vehicle with the young actress to head back to their accommodation.

I stayed on for the final setup of the night. By then, it was bitterly cold. Paul Cronin, as the motorcycle cop, was in full uniform; hard hat, jodhpurs and metal-capped boots. He was to run down the road, presumably in pursuit of Daniel and the girl. He clip-clopped along in those boots. His task was to stop suddenly in front of the 16mm film camera (the standard for location shoots in those days), strike a dramatic 'now I'm listening' pose, then run off past the lens. A classic telly move.

"ACTION!" someone yelled (oh, how I grew to love that word).

Cronin sprinted towards the camera and stopped, only to have his boots slide out from beneath him. Legs splayed, he landed flat on his back in what looked like a rather painful fall. One of those bruised or broken coccyx moments. *Ouch*. The crew rushed to help him up and hobbled him over to a caravan. I guess he recovered because *Matlock* went on for quite some time after that.

By then, I was the last member of the local public still watching. Everyone else had gone home. I was freezing, but utterly transfixed. I watched the dynamic between crew and cast, listened to a man I thought was the director calling out instructions. Years later, I

Are You Thinking What I'm Thinking? A Patchwork Journey Through My Life... So Far

discovered on IMDb that it was Tom Burstall, who was assistant director, managing the small, focused crew on set.

It's only now I realise how small the crew was. Maybe twenty people milling about, each playing their part. These days, a location shoot might involve up to two hundred crew members, dozens of trucks, traffic management, unit bases, catering... back then, it was stripped back and intimate.

The Burstall family was well known in the Australian film industry for years, and, coincidentally, Tom's lovely, creative, and passionate mother, Betty, had been my pottery teacher at Eltham High. Her pottery shed was iconic.

Tom had noticed me standing there, shivering but too enchanted to leave. As I finally turned to go, he acknowledged me with a brief wave, and I returned it before sauntering off into the short but shadowy bush path that led home. I was full of wonder and excitement. It was almost dreamlike.

I somehow *knew*, even then, that this was a life-changing moment. One of those "crux" moments Christopher Hitchens talks about. I couldn't fully recognise it, couldn't properly process or name it at the time. But it was real.

It would be fully understood some twenty years later, as I approached graduation from NIDA. But in hindsight, that night remains a crystal-clear snapshot burnt into my psyche of where my life was heading.

I had found my path. I had found my people.

A creative storytelling team, with a camera, a tight script, and some actors, doing it like it was real.

Are You Thinking What I'm Thinking?
A Patchwork Journey Through My Life... So Far

Music

Sweet music...

The soundtrack of my life.

The ever-present confirmation that there is beauty, art, expression, rebellion, joy, anger, love, regret, hope and confusion. All the wild and tender breadth of the human condition captured and carried through sonic waves, arranged and delivered in a way that feels like it was made just for me.

Despite the pain of living.

Other people get what they get from music, but the effect it has on me is deeply personal, utterly mine. It resonates with emotion, sharpens decision-making, clarifies thoughts, untangles feelings. It distracts when I need escape, provides a calm backdrop when the noise of life grows too loud. It can lift me into action, shift my mood, encourage, comfort, inspire, question... or affirm.

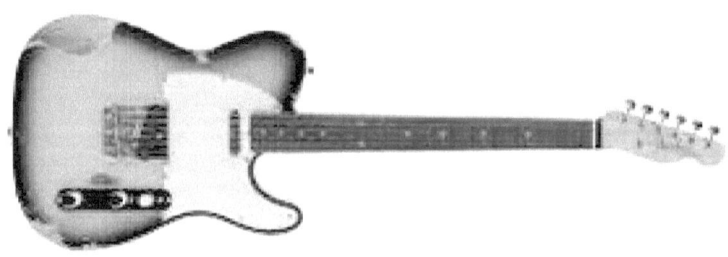

A worn Fender Telecaster... pure rock n roll

Are You Thinking What I'm Thinking? A Patchwork Journey Through My Life... So Far

The Blues

The bloke who lived across the road from us when I was a kid in Research was a bit of a bad boy. Jack. He and his Kiwi partner, Chris, had a turbulent relationship. Rows and tension were a regular occurrence between them. But despite that or perhaps because of it they seemed to take a bit of a shine to me. At least, I think they did. I used to hang around their place, probably far more than I should have.

Once I hit my teens, I was desperate to minimise my time at home. Hormones were kicking in, I had growing disdain for the parental role-modelling I was experiencing, and I felt a powerful urge to stretch out, grow up, get out, find my way in the world. I was also in the middle of experimenting with my identity, trying on different personas like outfits in a dressing room.

My brother confronted me one day with a derisive, 'What are you, Ken a lad or a hippy?'

I should've answered, 'I don't know yet I'm trying them all on.'

So I drifted over to Jack's whenever I could. He had this old mono record player, scratchy and stubborn, but it worked. He'd spin Bob Dylan, a few obscure American folk albums, some Frank Zappa... and about five Muddy Waters records. He played them endlessly.

I'd never heard the blues before. Jack knew all the lyrics by heart. There were beers, there were joints, and there was this heady blend of Delta blues, personal reinvention, and a changing world. Songs like Got My Mojo Working, I'm Your Hoochie Coochie Man, She Moves Me, I Just Wanna Make Love to You, Standing Around Crying, and Mannish Boy blared out raw, masculine, defiant. These were authentic Southern blues from Louisiana and the Mississippi Delta, and they hit me like a revelation.

It was a glorious initiation.

Are You Thinking What I'm Thinking?
A Patchwork Journey Through My Life… So Far

The blues laid the foundation for where my musical taste would go and grow. From Muddy Waters I found BB King, Freddie King, Albert Collins… The blues had arrived in my world like a thunderclap.

Muddy said it best: There's another mule kickin' in your stall.

Muddy Waters

Are You Thinking What I'm Thinking? A Patchwork Journey Through My Life... So Far

Short Cut Road

Around this time, I'd have been about 16 I started hanging out with some muso types around the Eltham area. It was a natural expression of the times, the living soundtrack of our youth. Music was everywhere, enveloping us, echoing our emotions, jiving and gliding us through life, all while heralding and supporting the socio-cultural shifts that swept through like a tsunami.

Every generation says, *"Oh, it used to be so much better."* But the truth is it really was.

As helpful as the internet and the World Wide Web were when they first arrived, they've since drained so much creative and developmental energy from our daily lives. Kids now *create* digitally because it's all they know. The digital world is so bloody instant. The tactile, physical act of creativity making art with your hands, learning an instrument, sketching an idea is now the exception rather than the norm among young people in the Western world.

It's not the kids' fault. They didn't invent this reality. Had it been around when I was their age, I'd have been just as hooked on gaming and social media as any of them. But it wasn't. We made our own fun, forged our own stories. Bands were popping up everywhere, lessons were being taken, garage doors were rattling with noise, music was happening!

I can't quite recall the first time I found the courage to sing where people could actually hear me. I rehearsed mostly in the shower. Forty-five-minute showers, belting out every word of *Mad Dogs & Englishmen* or *L.A. Woman*, singing along with the best in the world.

Maybe the first time I really sang out loud, properly, was in Roy Webb's loungeroom on Short Cut Road, Eltham. Roy was and still is a gatherer of people. A musical anchor. He's still playing, still connected to the scene. He and his wife, Sue, have maintained a long and beautiful bond both personally and through their shared love of blues, folk, and country music.

Are You Thinking What I'm Thinking?
A Patchwork Journey Through My Life… So Far

That's where it began. A band was formed. Rehearsals were organised. We named ourselves *Short Cut Road*, after the street that had brought us together. Somehow, I became the singer.

And I loved it.

Collaborating with like-minded souls, crafting tunes, building something real. It felt like I'd come home, found mycalling. Our sound was a mix of blues, folk, a bit of soul, a touch of country rock. We played a handful of small gigs, muddled our way through the usual growing pains: personality clashes, creative friction, drunken disagreements. But through it all, we made fabulous music.

Singin' a little blues with Short Cut Road

Over the next couple of years, I sang with a band called *Republic*. The driving force behind it was a fella named Calvyn Darragh a talented and prolific songwriter with a gift for crafting poppy, commercial tunes. We recorded a couple of demos at Richmond Recorders, which was one of the hottest studios around at the time.

Are You Thinking What I'm Thinking? A Patchwork Journey Through My Life… So Far

Decades later, those two songs resurfaced on a worn-out cassette, which I've since had digitised and saved. They're great tracks. Tight, catchy and full of promise.

Republic played a handful of small gigs, but we never really gained traction in terms of mainstream 'success'. Still, we had our moments.

One standout from that period was Mark Smith, a blazing guitarist who'd come down from Sydney. He blew us all away with his sheer skill and flair. He played the solos on those recordings. Brilliant, expressive work that still astonishes me every time I listen. A great player.

Fast forward to 2014–15, and I reconnected with Mark in Castlemaine. We teamed up again for a little while, playing small gigs mostly made up of songs from the great John Hiatt. The chemistry was still there. As a bonus, we also did a bit of building work together. On the tools by day, on the tunes by night.

Mark is the full package: a fabulous guitarist and an 'above average' carpenter. My kinda guy!

Are You Thinking What I'm Thinking?
A Patchwork Journey Through My Life... So Far

Sneak Preview

Back in the late 1970s, there was a weekly rock industry newspaper called Juke. It was brimming with advertisements for music shops, album and live gig reviews, gig listings, and a section dedicated to bands seeking members or musicians looking to make connections. One band, Sneak Preview, was on the lookout for a singer, so I decided to call for an audition. They were a tight-knit, four-on-the-floor rockin' outfit needing a front man. Two guitars, bass, drums with echoes of Thin Lizzy and the stadium rockers of the era. This was a time when the live music scene in Melbourne was pumping. To my delight, they seemed to like me and invited me to join. They were the most professional band I had played with up to that point.

So here I am, fronting this band. A rock star in the making? Perhaps!

The music was tight and punchy, with the duelling guitars of Ken Sheppard and Dominic Morabito being both familiar and expertly played. Mark Sachs provided a solid and straightforward bass line, anchoring the bottom end, while Peter Robertson, who is still performing with the great Mike Rudd, delivered fabulous, appropriate feels and fills on the drums. We were gigging regularly! We secured a manager! We even had a road crew! For about two years, we played between three and five gigs a week. We were a mid-tier support band for Premier Artists, the booking agency that organised all the gigs. This meant we would headline on Wednesdays or Thursdays at both suburban and inner-city venues, and on weekends, we would support acts like Australian Crawl, Men At Work, The Divinyls and Jo Jo Zep and The Falcons.

We passed rough demos to Mike Brady, known for "Up There Cazaly" and countless commercial jingles, as he was searching for a hot rock band for his new Full Moon Records label. He liked what he heard and invited us to record demos at his newly acquired Flagstaff Studios in Melbourne. It was a fantastic experience.

Are You Thinking What I'm Thinking? A Patchwork Journey Through My Life… So Far

Brady was impressed with one of our songs and offered us a deal for a single. We signed the contract and recorded "I Never Thought" sometime in 1980. I co-wrote the track with Dominic Morabito, one of our talented guitarists. The single sold approximately 400 copies and briefly made it into the top 100. I eventually received two cheques for royalties from this record: one for performance payment, amounting to $17 AUD, and the second for half of the songwriting royalties, which was $34 AUD. This starkly illustrates the financial disparity between being Pete Townshend and Roger Daltrey, the writer and the performer.

I believe this is why bands like U2 and the Red Hot Chili Peppers choose to split everything equally among their members. The essence of collaboration is paramount, isn't it? Being underappreciated is challenging enough in life, business, or art, but for many band members over the years, the distribution of royalty payments has been grossly unfair. The individual who writes the lyrics or creates the melody often reaps all the financial rewards for the piece. What about the saxophonist who contributed that memorable hook? Or the guitarist who crafted that signature phrase and solo? And what of the distinctive singer who added so much to the overall sound? An inequitable distribution of earnings can easily drive a wedge into any professional relationship.

Sneak Preview

Are You Thinking What I'm Thinking?
A Patchwork Journey Through My Life... So Far

John Farnham

We recorded our tracks for the record deal in Studio No. 2 at Armstrong Audio Visual in South Melbourne, a major studio where countless bands had laid down their music. The recording experience was a mixed bag, with Mike Brady at the helm as producer. He softened the A-side considerably, shortening it and adding Wendy Stapleton for backing vocals. He completely replaced Peter's strong drum beats with 'Coxy', the session drummer, which was a blow to Peter, as he had a fantastic feel and understood the style perfectly. Brady essentially 'middle-of-the-roaded' our sound.

One night during the recording sessions, I was the last band member to leave the studio. Mike Brady had asked Graham Goble from the Little River Band, who was producing in Studio One, if I could sit in the control room for a while. John Farnham was recording vocals for his comeback album, 'Uncovered'. As I entered the plush, expansive control room, I realised I was in the presence of serious players in the music industry. Goble acknowledged me, invited me to sit on the large leather couch positioned away from the massive mixing desk. John was in the studio, slightly turned towards us, with a single microphone in front of him. A baffle separated the mic from a foldback speaker aimed at him. He wasn't wearing headphones, apparently preferring to avoid them. Goble said, "Okay, let's give it a go."

What I observed and heard that day has been etched into my memory ever since. The single, simple piano chord that began the final verse of Farnham's iconic rendition of The Beatles' "Help". I was there, witnessing the power, emotion and phrasing that John delivered. It was nothing short of breathtaking. His voice possesses multiple harmonics, it is as if there are two people singing at once, the cracks and whistles enhancing the richness. It was one of the most extraordinary moments of my life. I was profoundly moved to see and hear this brilliant artist pouring everything he had into the material, as if his life depended on it. The freedom of expression, astonishing range, and fearless delivery were remarkable. John Farnham is a national treasure, and I felt incredibly fortunate to have been present for that moment. I thanked Graham and left the studio in a daze.

During that period, we performed at the Richmond Football Club, where there was a venue on Punt Road, right next to the footy ground and in the shadow of the mighty MCG. We were supporting Farnham around the time of the release of 'Uncovered'. Glenn Wheatley had taken on the management of John some time before. Among the members of his band that night were Tommy Emmanuel on guitar, Mal Logan on keys, and I believe the late, great Roger McLachlan was on bass. The music was classy and brilliant. We did our part as a solid support band, with an excellent sound system, nice lights, and a full house. We went down well, warming up the crowd for John and his band.

Just after our set, we were in the small band room allocated to us when Glenn Wheatley walked in. "Hey guys, that was great!" he said, smiling graciously. We exchanged pleasantries, and I remember thinking, "Thanks, Glenn, we think you're great too! Want to manage us?" But we didn't say it out loud. He smiled again and eased himself out the door. How do we follow that up? We wondered. I can't recall how we managed it, but he certainly didn't offer to take us under his wing.

Cold Chisel

In the winter of 1979, we scored a three-night support slot for Cold Chisel, who were the biggest live act in Australia at the time. We opened for them at two packed suburban venues, and then on the Saturday night, we played at the legendary Bombay Rock in Brunswick, Melbourne. At one of the venues, possibly The Waltzing Matilda or The Ferntree Gully Hotel, the place was absolutely jumping during our set from 8:30 to 9:30. The venues were bursting at the seams, and back then, smoking was allowed, everyone smoked. It was revolting. You'd walk in and your clothes would instantly reek of cigarettes, needing a thorough fumigation to rid them of the tobacco stench. Approaching any of these venues from the outside, it looked as

Are You Thinking What I'm Thinking?
A Patchwork Journey Through My Life... So Far

if the place was on fire, with smoke billowing out through the doors. It sounds impossible given today's strict regulations, but that was the reality.

As we reached the final song of our set, which I think was Robert Palmer's "You're Gonna Get What's Coming," the crowd was going wild... for us! The support act! I said 'thanks, but we gotta go', they were yelling for more! Traditionally, if one person called for an encore, we'd do it! We gave 'em their money's worth, we were a hardworking band. 'Thank you!' Fist in the air as we were about to leave the stage. They continued to shout... Chisel's frontman and legendary Australian rocker, Jimmy Barnes, was on the side of the stage. "Fookin' do another one!" he yelled, physically pushing us back on. We obliged and launched into Thin Lizzy's "Rosalie." What a night it was, truly the gig of a lifetime for me. Barnsey was hooting with delight as we left the stage. What a guy! Typically, the main act only gives you a fraction of the lights and about half the power of the PA, but Chisel provided us with a heap of both.

Fast forward to the year 2000, I found myself in the green room on level five of Stadium Australia during the closing ceremony of the Olympic Games, high up in the grandstand. I was there with the cast of Bananas, along with four other 'Australian icons'. The five of us did a lap of the stadium on specially made floats, Bananas (who received the biggest cheers!), Kylie, Paul Hogan as Mick Dundee, Elle McPherson, and golfer Greg Norman. The applause was rapturous! Then, the Bananas danced with Kylie as she performed one of her hits, probably "Locomotion," though I can't be certain. It was the longest time Nicholas and I had ever spent in the costumes. It was a hot night in Sydney, and we were working our butts off.

After the performance, the costume department freed us from those heat chambers down in one of the vomitories (the entrances to the stadium), and we found ourselves surrounded by some of the world's best athletes, all holding out pens and paper, eager for autographs from the fruit. "Wait! You're the heroes!"

Are You Thinking What I'm Thinking? A Patchwork Journey Through My Life... So Far

Jimmy Barnes was also at the closing ceremony, singing "Working Class Man" and completely lifting the imaginary ceiling off the stadium. With 100,000 people in attendance, it was the biggest gig ever.

During the afternoon rehearsal, I had a chat with Jimmy in the green room. I said, "I'm thinking you won't remember this, Jim, but I want to thank you for something you did in 1979." I recounted the story of him pushing us to play an encore. He replied, "You're right, I don't remember. But I'm glad you're telling me. We always looked after our support bands because we were treated like shit when we were a support." Then he asked for a Banana autograph for the Tin Lids (his kids). Swings and roundabouts…

BIP cast spreading the love at the Olympic Games after Barnsey had warmed them up for us. Sydney, 2000

The thrill of performance

Fronting Sneak Preview was an incredible experience for me. The discipline and focus required to deliver high-energy shows in varying conditions, at odd times of day and in dodgy locations, truly builds character. All the band members had day jobs: Mark was a cabinet maker, Ken worked as a printer, Dominic was a flamboyant hairdresser, and I was on the tools as a carpenter's mate or bricklayer's

Are You Thinking What I'm Thinking?
A Patchwork Journey Through My Life… So Far

labourer. I can't recall what Peter did for a living. We worked tirelessly, balancing our jobs, rehearsing, driving, recovering, and somehow trying to pull it all together. Being in the band actually cost us money. Yes, we were paid for gigs, but all the earnings went to the road crew, with a portion allocated to management. I don't know if this is entirely accurate, but I remember it costing me about $2,000 a year to be part of the band. That's rock 'n' roll for you.

We disbanded in 1980 or '81, our last gig was on a Saturday night at some coastal venue. The place was packed with off-their-faces surfers doing the cockroach on the floor in front of us. I vividly recall one particularly brainless individual tipping an ashtray into his mouth and chewing it down the front, pure class. There was broken glass on the floor, and drunk idiots were doing their thing. We couldn't wait for it to end.

During this time, I had begun taking part-time acting classes at a small school in St Kilda called the Peggy Rush School of Acting. Peggy later suggested I audition for NIDA, which I had never heard of before. Sneak Preview had done its job; we gave it our best shot, and the prospect of NIDA started to look very promising.

Here's a significant takeaway for me: nothing compares to the thrill of performing tight music at a great venue when the band is on fire, the sound mix is excellent, and the crowd is going wild. The joy of that experience is unique, almost otherworldly, and unmatched in all the other areas I've worked in. Thank you, Sneak Preview… Rock and roll will never die!

Are You Thinking What I'm Thinking? A Patchwork Journey Through My Life... So Far

Belting it out with Sneak Preview in a packed Melbourne 'beer barn.'

Jazz

I became deeply enamoured with jazz in the early 1990s when my partner at the time, Rita, began playing with a fantastic group called The Umbrellas. They travelled extensively throughout New South Wales and parts of Victoria, performing Musica Viva concerts in schools. These highly skilled and talented musicians moved from school to school, engaging students by introducing them to jazz, discussing the nuances of feel, the structure of music, melody, harmony, and improvisation. They even collaborated with the students to create music. What a remarkable learning experience for these kids! They were in the presence of exceptional musicians, witnessing the skill, discipline, and, indeed, the freedom of music-making at its finest.

This period was life-changing for me in many ways, most notably, we had a new baby, Georgia! From a musical perspective, it was an incredible learning curve. The broad and wonderful world of jazz opened up to me, with this band serving as the catalyst. I was fortunate to be present many times when these musicians improvised, communicated through their instruments, and truly listened to one another. Oh, the importance of listening in jazz, and in all music! Jazz has become an integral part of my daily life now, without fail. It reflects and supports whatever the vibe is throughout the day, morning, noon, or night, there's always jazz for the occasion.

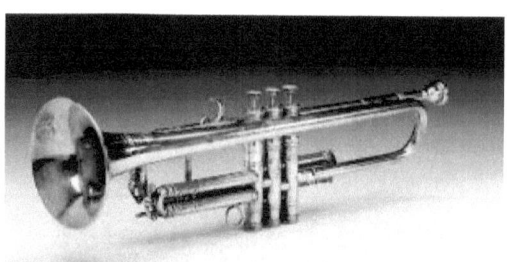

Cool jazz trumpet is currently my favourite solo instrument but hey, the next funky middle 8 could change that…

The Power of The Dog

In 2020, when Covid struck in a significant way, I landed a small, yet pivotal role (they're all pivotal if I'm playing them!) in the Academy Award-winning film directed by Jane Campion, The Power of the Dog. The picture was shot in Otago on New Zealand's South Island, which they somehow transformed to resemble the Rockies in Montana circa 1910. Many of the interior scenes were filmed in a studio in Auckland. The entire experience was quite dramatic for me; the Victorian government was about to announce a Covid lockdown at 5:30 in the afternoon on the day I was scheduled to fly. This would have meant I could not travel to New Zealand after that announcement. Consequently, production arranged for a car to pick me up, and I had secured permission for leave without pay from my teaching job. The car raced me to the airport, and I managed to secure the last available seat on an Air New Zealand flight to Christchurch. Everything worked out, and I arrived safely. I loved it.

I was fortunate enough to work with Jane for the first time, alongside some lovely people, including the wonderful Gen Lemon, whom I've

Are You Thinking What I'm Thinking? A Patchwork Journey Through My Life… So Far

known for many years and collaborated with several times. Sean Keenan, the actor and heartthrob, was great fun, and all the American cowboys were a hoot, of course. I had pleasant, easy conversations with Jesse Plemons. The other American and British stars were cordial, professional, and suitably inclusive, what more could you ask for? I don't need to be everyone's best friend; we are there to work.

Fame and celebrity seem to hold significant importance for students and people in general. They often ask, "Who's the most famous person you've worked with?" and "Are you famous? Are you a celebrity?" Fame is often regarded as an important or at least interesting concept. Not for me! We're here to work! I don't care if you're the ever-smiling Mary Tyler Moore, the intense Julie Christie, the enigmatic Benedict Cumberbatch, Johnny Depp, or the regal Cate Blanchett, I've worked with them all, and we're just working!

Covid heavily disrupted the shoot of The Power of the Dog of course. I filmed one scene before production was shut down for six weeks. I had already completed two weeks of isolation in New Zealand, but I was allowed to fly back to Australia to undergo another two weeks of isolation. When I returned to film my remaining scenes, I had to complete two more weeks of isolation at either end. In total, I spent seven weeks in isolation for what I estimate to be about 30 seconds of screen time, half of which is in the dark. It's glamorous, it's sparkling, it's ego-boosting! I'm famous! Not! But I loved the experience, I always love working. I always have. I feel more at home on a film set than in any other workplace. It's my passion; it doesn't feel like work at all, it's like a kind of juice for living.

Jane Campion is a remarkable director and writer; she won the Academy Award for Best Director for The Power of the Dog. It was the first film directed by a woman to be nominated for 12 Academy Awards. Jane is also the first woman to be nominated twice for Best Director, having received a nomination for The Piano and winning the Oscar for Best Screenplay in 1994 for the same film. Her screenwriting is briliant, deeply cinematic. You can visualise the screen as you read.

Are You Thinking What I'm Thinking?
A Patchwork Journey Through My Life... So Far

You find yourself asking, "What happens next?" as you engage with her work. You can see, hear, and feel the location, the action, and the vibe as you read. Her writing carries you along and 'creates' the film in your mind.

With Sean Keenan and Jane Campion, The Power of The Dog, 2021

The arrival of the script, the welcome pack, production info...

Years ago, prior to the dominance of digital technology, all actors in a film would receive a copy of the script, regardless of the size of their role. As a matter of professional courtesy and collaboration, a hard copy of the script would arrive by courier, very personal, private and

Are You Thinking What I'm Thinking? A Patchwork Journey Through My Life... So Far

discreet; often accompanied by a handwritten note from the producer or director, or both, welcoming you to the production and thanking you for your involvement. This was a wonderful part of the creative team-building process, making you feel truly engaged.

Opening the securely sealed bag and physically extracting the A4 envelopes filled with production information, sometimes including a crew and cast list, accommodation details, timeframes, and scheduling information, all printed on letterhead and smelling fresh, was exhilarating. It signified that I was working. Here began my valued contribution. At that moment, I was 100% involved. I could finally settle into my preparation processes. All that research, reflection, backstory preparation, and physical conditioning could be safely compartmentalised, ready to draw upon as needed. Now, I could smell the script, read it, and immerse myself in the journey of the story. (First, I'd quickly read through all my parts to see how much I was actually involved of course.)

However, these days, unless you are a reasonably significant character, you only receive your scenes via email. This feels rather impersonal and somewhat withholding. It's as if they're saying, "You're a bit-part player, mate; here's your bit." It doesn't matter how much experience or quality you bring to the piece; you're simply given your lines. I understand the reasoning behind this, but honestly, it was better the old way.

This time, however, on The power of the Dog, production accidentally emailed me the entire shooting script! I settled in with a glass or two of brilliant New Zealand red wine in my hotel and immersed myself in the screenplay. I found myself physically and vocally responding to so much as I navigated my way through this brilliant work. By the end, I was breathless, gazing out at a bright New Zealand night, feeling full, available, valuable, and inspired. It was a wonderful moment, a true page-turner! (Remember when we used to actually turn pages?) A day later, I received an email from production asking me to return the script. "Too bloody late!" I chuckled. "I've read the whole thing!" I

Are You Thinking What I'm Thinking?
A Patchwork Journey Through My Life... So Far

knew they were just following legal protocol, but I was following the storytelling process, "Deliver, and I shall read!"

On set, Jane is, of course, fantastic. I'm eagerly awaiting her call for the next project. I'm pretty sure she'll need a rough-headed 'character actor' to enhance her next production. I'm ready. If you accidentally send me the script, I'm perfectly fine with that.

Isotunes

While in New Zealand, I bought a ¾ size red guitar that I could play in my hotel room during my isolation. I kept it with me throughout the entire period. I started playing some tunes, many of which were penned by John Hiatt, a musician I greatly admire. I recorded videos of the tunes on my iPhone, shared a little story before each one, and posted them on Facebook. At the time, I was living a rather lonesome existence, even more so than usual, so these tunes provided a great way to stay active and creative. I was also teaching classes remotely in Media, Drama, and Acting via Google Classroom, which is actually a fantastic teaching tool. In the end, I think I uploaded around 27 tunes, pretty ordinary quality, but hey! They were challenging times!

Those videos are still available on my Facebook page under 'Isotunes', some of them even went viral, racking up 34 or 35 views! Crazy! It was a great period; yes, Covid was challenging for us all, but there was something about it that appealed to me, I can't quite put my finger on it. Perhaps I enjoy uncertainty? Being alone? I'll have to ask my therapist... oh, that's right, I stopped seeing him a couple of years ago. Maybe I should schedule a top-up visit to see how he's doing.

Are You Thinking What I'm Thinking? A Patchwork Journey Through My Life... So Far

The little red one! For ISOtunes

Driving. Four wheels and a full tank

I don't care about pollution.

I'm an air-conditioned gypsy.

That's my solution.

Watch the Police and the taxman miss me I'm mobile!

(Going Mobile, Who's Next – The Who 1971)

I have always loved driving, even before I could actually get behind the wheel. In 1964 or 1965, my parents owned a fairly new FC Holden. Everything about it: the smell, the look of the dashboard, the deep, almost translucent crimson of the steering wheel centre, and the proud Holden Lion emblem, head held high and ready for action!

My father was a bit of a grumpy driver, while my mother was quite frightening behind the wheel, she always drove flat out, lacking the skill to back it up. She stacked every car we owned. She chain-smoked as she drove; everyone seemed to smoke back then. In banks, restaurants, on aircraft, in hospitals, doctor's waiting rooms, supermarkets, trains, and cinemas, smoking was ubiquitous. My mother was a chain smoker for at least forty years.

Are You Thinking What I'm Thinking?
A Patchwork Journey Through My Life… So Far

FC Holden

Driving has always represented a ticket to freedom for me, even back then, I must have been about seven years old. I remember sitting in the car parked in the driveway, glancing down to see the keys in the ignition! The turning mechanism was complicated, involving several positions followed by a push action, and then the final turn would engage the starter motor to fire up the engine. I looked out at my parents, who were fully immersed in some task in the front yard. After a few practice attempts, I decided to go all the way to see what would happen.

Things happened. The starter motor engaged; the car lurched forward up the driveway in a bunny-hop, kangaroo fashion, kershug, kershug, kershug! I was too shocked to release my grip on the ignition. My dad ran towards the car, and as he did, I sort of rolled over to the passenger side on the deep red bench seat, finally letting go of the wheel and the ignition switch. Thankfully, the car didn't fully fire up; it just lurched a few times up the drive with the young freedom seeker behind the wheel. "Don't ever turn the car on!" my dear old dad firmly instructed. "Thank Christ it was in gear," I heard him mutter to my relieved mother.

Thus, my journey behind the wheel spluttered to a start. I have driven approximately 500,000 km in my life, averaging 200 km per week for 50 years at a minimum. This includes work commutes, and from 2002, access weekends/holidays with my older kids Georgia and Angus. Then from 2008 Sydney/Melbourne returns on School holidays to

Are You Thinking What I'm Thinking? A Patchwork Journey Through My Life... So Far

collect and drop Marvin and Angelica. The kids and me spent a lot of time travelling! Eating snacks, listening to great music, watching both movies and the world go by. I shudder to think how much fuel I've consumed.

I've been called an 'overthinker'... let me ponder that

I rarely, if ever, think in an ordered, linear fashion where I weigh up pros and cons, critically approach an issue, run through a checklist, or balance facts and probabilities against projections. No, my thoughts inevitably resemble a jumbled cloud, a loose stream of consciousness bubbling around in a familiar chaotic mess. Sometimes, I might practice or rehearse what I want to say or what I should have said to someone. There's often a merry-go-round of hope, regret, sex, fear, practice, food, hope, regret, sex, sex, fear, rehearsal, food, sex... hope. I do feel a little quietly virtuous when I stumble upon a session of reasonably ordered, one might say, productive thought processes. "Yes! You covered some ground there, mate. Got a little something done, Kenneth." Now, how shall I reward myself?

A little ozone depletion on Research oval

Are You Thinking What I'm Thinking?
A Patchwork Journey Through My Life... So Far

Leaping into action as Nicholas (B2) wonders if this guy will ever get it right. Producer/Director Virginia Lumsden looks on deciding if there is a diplomatic way forward.

Sidney Myer Music Bowl, Melbourne. 1995

With 50,000 people in attendance, it was the same exhilarating atmosphere as the Parramatta gig; the crowd went absolutely wild! It was bigger than Jesus for four-year-olds! In the midst of this chaos, B2's pants fell down, he'll do anything to pull focus! He blamed it on a wardrobe malfunction. Meanwhile, B1 didn't flinch. He took control and kept the show pumping while the costume staff fussed about with the 'support fruit's' issues.

I mean really, B1 carried B2 over so much rocky ground, never seeking glory for himself. He was always there for the team, consistently covering, supporting, helping, counselling, and saving! I'm always here for you, B2!

Cars

I learned to drive in a 1948 FX Holden paddock bomb owned by Robin Pocock, the kid next door. We would all pile into the FX, and Robin would tear down the driveway in a dramatic fashion. I watched him like a Hawk, as he handled the accelerator, clutch, and the three-on-the-tree gear shift. He was a skilled driver, always tearing down the driveway, racing car style. Eventually, he let me have a go and guided me through the process of getting the car rolling. Oh wow... my world

Are You Thinking What I'm Thinking? A Patchwork Journey Through My Life… So Far

opened up. I excitedly told my mum and dad that I could now drive and needed to start reversing the cars out of our driveway.

My lead-footed mother had a dark blue VW Beetle that she adored, and so did I. They allowed me to drive it up the hill to the Research footy oval, which was quiet and rarely saw any traffic. I would take the VW up there and zip around the dirt road for hours, going round and round in my mum's Bug. I would push it on the corners, drifting sideways and revving through the gears. I learned to handle dirt, dust, and gravel roads. Sometimes, I would park near the Scout Hall and just sit there, daydreaming about driving, freedom, girls, football, and music… simply sitting in the car. While some guys went fishing, I found solace in the car. I don't know why; it just happened that way. Occasionally, I would spend an extended period gazing into my own eyes in the rear-view mirror, like a full-frame, cinematic shot of my eyes. What was I searching for? Trying to penetrate through the cornea and delve into the even denser mush of my frontal lobe? Hello! Is there anything in there, Kenneth? Any rhyme or reason presenting itself for you, mate? After a while… apparently not. Better do a few more laps of the park.

Vehicles, fuel usage, the wind in my hair (yes… I had plenty!) have been significant aspects of my life. Throughout this work, I'm randomly including a selection of vehicles, motorcycles, and accompanying stories as we meander along the road of my reflections.

1949 FX Holden   1969 VW Beetle

Are You Thinking What I'm Thinking?
A Patchwork Journey Through My Life... So Far

Holden 1964 EH wagon

My first car was purchased in 1975, shortly after I turned 18 and obtained my licence! I failed my first attempt at the Eltham Police Station. The constable didn't appreciate that I had my elbow out of the window and changed gears in my Mum's Bug as if I were a bloody racing driver. However, I managed to pass a week later when I had woken up to myself a bit. The EH cost $600 from Wayne Tesch, a champion Eltham footy player. It was white, with a three-on-the-tree gear shift and an orange billiard ball on the gear stick.

I fashioned a large block of foam rubber into a bed in the back. My girlfriend at the time made some red curtains for privacy when we went down to the beach and slept in the car, listening to the waves crash and the music of the day through the state-of-the-art Pioneer tape system. The Eagles, The Dingoes, Van Morrison, Joe Cocker, Renee Geyer, Free, Janis Joplin, Jimi Hendrix, Blood, Sweat & Tears, Bob Dylan, Led Zeppelin, The Who, Ariel, Chicago, Little River Band, Jethro Tull... and more. Fuel was cheap, and there was hardly any traffic on the roads back then. But the road toll was horrifically high, drink driving was rampant. If you could find your keys, you could have a go at driving home. 3,694 people lost their lives on Australian roads in 1975. Yet, there was freedom, music, love, and plenty of weed. The weed back then was nowhere near as potent as it is today, so a little joint would give you a happy little glow rather than blow your brains out, which isn't really any fun anyway. Every road in Australia felt like it was potentially mine. With four wheels, a full tank, a pocket full of confidence (cash!), and a weekend ahead, the possibilities were endless.

Are You Thinking What I'm Thinking? A Patchwork Journey Through My Life... So Far

Vespa 125cc (1959)

I bought it for 50 bucks from Brian Hurst, sheesh, I wish I had it now! It would fetch tens of thousands! I was just 13 at the time, and that's when my love of motorcycling began!

Vespa 1959 125   *Holden 1964 EH Wagon*

Are You Thinking What I'm Thinking?
A Patchwork Journey Through My Life… So Far

First steps 1958

Calling the kitty. Johnny Shielly
The Harp in The South, 1986

I know… I was researching the role, even then… method guy.

My first memory and some more…

I fell into a trench. Really, that's my earliest memory. I must have been about 3 or 4 years old, around 1960 or 1961. There was a substantial secondary carriageway a little way from our house on Summerhill Road in Reservoir, called Crevelli Street. It was quite steep and ran all the way down, past the Crevelli Street shops, and continued on to Preston Northeast Primary School. Somewhere down there was a doctor's clinic. On this particular day, I was with my mother, who I believe had an appointment. I was in the waiting room, and as a curious youngster, I made my way to the exit door and wandered out through the open gate.

Young Kenneth decided to investigate the trench outside the clinic, perhaps a kind of early archaeological exploration? Unfortunately, he fell in. There was a piece of sharp tin sticking out of the wall of the

Are You Thinking What I'm Thinking? A Patchwork Journey Through My Life... So Far

trench, and I sliced my little finger on it quite severely. I don't remember the stitches, the pain, or much of the incident apart from falling in and screaming for my mother. It was fortuitous to be outside the clinic, as the nasty gash was attended to immediately. I bore the scar for many years and ended up with a slightly crooked pinkie as a result. That is my earliest memory.

A couple of years later, I encountered Crevelli Street again, literally. This time, I was on an old scooter. Down, down, down I hurtled at breakneck speed. I recall the 'death wobbles' beginning. Those of you who have experienced the death wobbles will understand that there's no stopping them. It took a discarded half-brick lying in the gutter to abruptly halt my descent. Over the handlebars I went, sailing through the air! Crevelli Street came up fast to greet me, leaving quite a bit of itself embedded in my stomach, chest, thighs, hands, and face. I took off quite a bit of bark and remember the pain of the pieces of bitumen being removed with tweezers.

A few days later, I was home from school and vomiting terribly. My mother thought it seemed rather serious and took me to the Austin Hospital. That's when I was diagnosed with viral meningitis. Being viral, it could not be treated with drugs; it needed to run its course. And it did. I missed a lot of school, returning even more isolated and lacking in confidence than before. This illness can have significant or even catastrophic effects on sufferers, who can indeed die, but one can also be left with various forms of brain damage. So, it wasn't a particularly high point for my physical and perhaps mental health.

I recall that I wrote a card to the nurse I had fallen in love with, Miss Vagg, after I was released. (A romantic at six?) I was told my writing was completely in mirror style, as if the reader were looking into a mirror. She was the nurse who held my hand and stroked my head while I endured multiple lumbar punctures. They needed to extract fluid and have it checked, and apparently, you had to be conscious for these. She told me I was very brave. I loved her. I trusted her. Thanks to Miss Vagg's positive support, I remained 'brave' through medical procedures and in the dentist's chair for decades afterward. I am less brave now. I've grown weary of bits of me being cut out and sent to pathology. It is sheer luck that the relentless Australian sun has not claimed me, as it has so many others with the dreaded skin cancer. Be thankful, Kenneth… and I am. Daily… even if it's just a little bit.

Evidence based behavioural Psych exploration can be fun!

I didn't attend kindergarten. I'm not sure why. There must be some reason that eludes me. By that time, I was already grappling with a heavily compromised attachment to my mother, and my sister not living with us cast a profound, permanent, unstable, and sad shadow over our family. Then, at barely four and a half years of age, this unsure child was taken to Preston Northeast Primary to begin Prep. I was far from ready. On top of the mixed messages I was receiving from my mother, I was wholly unsocialised, having had no childcare or kindergarten experience. I remember crying and crying, being left out in the hallway at school for reasons I can only guess at, shaking with fear and feelings of abandonment. It was painfully obvious to me that my mother had dumped me. I was frightened, feeling stupid and

Are You Thinking What I'm Thinking? A Patchwork Journey Through My Life... So Far

unlovable. I hated school; It exposed the dummy I thought I was. My cognitive capabilities and ability to negotiate simple patterns were low, which compromised my understanding and development in Maths and English. All of this, coupled with the underlying banishment of my sister, which I will elaborate on soon, formed the precarious foundation upon which my coping mechanisms were built throughout early childhood. This would influence my emotional development, academic capacity, relationship-building, and behaviour for decades to come.

I now understand that these coping and survival instincts manifest in all of us in various ways, depending on DNA, ancestry, parental influence, trauma, siblings, and environmental factors. I remember being enveloped in a cloud of depression and worry during my first three years of primary school. Those were very difficult years for this little fair-skinned, red-headed boy.

Behavioural psychology should be an ongoing and well-taught component of our education system. It should be a behavioural journey of discovery, integrated into the curriculum. Age-appropriate, fun, light-hearted, and accompanied by a dollop of humour and irony, it should be taught in a way that helps children grasp and accept these concepts. Numerous university and clinical studies have undoubtedly been conducted on these matters.

Why are we the way we are?

If we could incorporate this understanding as a natural ingredient in our learning, parallel to academic, sports, and creative studies, then perhaps the behaviour of our friends, those we interact with, our families, and indeed ourselves, might be easier to comprehend. This ongoing study, as a natural inclusion in our education, coupled with consistent lessons on acceptance, empathy, and compassion, would be immensely beneficial in the schools I've worked at. History might make more sense, and civics could be grasped in a more real-world context. Storytelling, English, poetry, literature, theatre, and film would take on deeper meaning and layered investigation. The human

Are You Thinking What I'm Thinking?
A Patchwork Journey Through My Life... So Far

condition could be explored endlessly, much like the peeling of an onion, as Peer Gynt asks, "But where is the core?"

Is there a core? Does it matter? Why? What is actually important?

Did I mention philosophy? I will now…

Philosophy! Let's integrate that into the curriculum while we're at it!

My Mother, the multitudinal Joyce Radley

Are You Thinking What I'm Thinking? A Patchwork Journey Through My Life... So Far

Young Kenneth, (reflective?) Father Donald Radley and brother Peter

Are You Thinking What I'm Thinking?
A Patchwork Journey Through My Life… So Far

The Radley troops, on one of the rare but welcome occasions we hook up.

John and Peter in front. Myself and Jane in the rear.

Closing ceremony of the Olympic Games, Sydney 2000.

One hundred thousand people this time, Bananas, Bananas! The entire cast was on a float, doing a glory lap of the running track alongside four other Australian icons on their own floats: Kylie, the most wonderful and gracious professional; Elle MacPherson, the former supermodel; Greg Norman, the golfer; and Paul Hogan as Mick Dundee. Around we went, giving it our all. That was the longest we had ever been in the suits, more than an hour, for goodness' sake! It was quite challenging. When we were finally led down through the vomitory and able to have those hot-as-hell heads removed, we were surrounded by hundreds of the world's top athletes wanting our autographs! What? Shouldn't it be the other way around? It was one of the greatest nights of my life. I loved signing fan cards for Barnsey and Vanessa Amorosi, and chatting with the gorgeous Kylie.

Are You Thinking What I'm Thinking? A Patchwork Journey Through My Life… So Far

The wonderful Kerry O'Dowd Haretuku leading us down the home straight of Stadium Australia.

Art can sneak up on us

In the late spring of 1983, on a lovely warm day in Sydney, a tiny yet remarkable moment occurred in the upstairs of 'Top Tote', the old jockey change rooms that we used as a movement studio and rehearsal space in High Street Kensington. The smell of the Morton Bay figs, the sound of galloping racehorses training, and the call of the Currawongs are still nestled in the forefront of my memory.

This was NIDA in the 1980s. We didn't fully appreciate that it was an extraordinary place to be; we were simply existing in the moment. Yet, it truly was an amazing environment. Baz Luhrmann smashed a window, Steven Berkoff arrived on a Kwaka 900, Vanessa Redgrave enchanted us, Jeremy Irons didn't realise his fly was undone, and Arky Michael shocked everyone with his cooking demonstration. I had even moved into Hugo Weaving's old room. It was a special time.

I was in the second year of my three-year diploma (which was later converted to a degree). On this particular day, one of my fellow students, Marcelle Schmitz, and I were set to perform our scene work for the Head of Acting, Nick Enright. We had chosen a scene between

Are You Thinking What I'm Thinking?
A Patchwork Journey Through My Life… So Far

Blanche and Mitch from the classic Tennessee Williams play, *A Streetcar Named Desire*. It was a wonderful scene where Blanche, in full steam with her damaged, poetic charm, engages with Mitch, who is breaking out into a flop sweat while maintaining a restrained, gentlemanly respect for this fascinating, exotic woman. It is a brilliant moment, superbly written. Both characters are deeply engaged in their individual journeys while seemingly connecting with each other.

Marcelle was somehow both fragile and strong, present yet distant, focused yet dreamy, a fine actor, absolutely nailing this moment. I think I did alright too, mesmerised by her presence and accepting both the sub-tropical air temperature and the dramatic heat in Top Tote.

We performed the scene, which was quite lengthy and had been prepared over an extended period. Finally, it came to its conclusion. We kept our heads down for a beat or two after the final moment, then slowly looked up at our tutor. He was wiping away tears. Nick had the most incredible, large pale blue eyes and a deep, soothing voice. "Thank you," was all he could say. We sat for a moment, then respectfully rose and left the space, making room for the next students to present their pieces. Marcelle quietly asked me, "Was he crying because we were good or bad?"

That was a significant 15 or 20 minutes for me. A brilliantly written scene that only one person witnessed, on a hot afternoon, in an upstairs room of what was then considered the premier actor training institution in the country. With an excellent actor opposite me and in the presence of one of the great contributors to Australian theatre, it's only upon reflection that this moment resonates so strongly. A small moment in the 1980s in Sydney.

Are You Thinking What I'm Thinking? A Patchwork Journey Through My Life… So Far

Early NIDA

Nick Enright

Cut to 35 years hence…

So, after many years and a remarkable journey in theatre, film, television, and now teaching, I find myself as the Director of the Ministry of Performing Arts College in Melbourne. There I was, in a spacious, bright rehearsal room/studio, working with some fabulously fit, bright-eyed, and passionate young musical theatre students who were preparing their performance pieces for their end-of-year showcase. I had been teaching, guiding, mentoring, and coaching, both directing and remaining silent with my students as required. We worked solidly all day, and I was continually impressed by their skill, passion, and energy. At the same time, I was coaxing, suggesting, questioning, guiding, challenging, and supporting them.

Great progress was occurring throughout the group. There were excellent performers among the cohort, and they would undoubtedly grow and refine their talents over the years. As the last scene finished, I was ready to pack up after a fulfilling, albeit slightly tiring day. "Then we go into the song," the actress informed me as the acting moment concluded. Throughout our studies, we had discussed the delightful moment in a musical when nothing else can occur but the song, that is why the song happens; because that is all that can happen now!

My brilliant colleague, Deb Mitchelmore, asked me if I had heard Caitlin (the actress) sing. "Not yet," I replied. Deb suggested we play the scene once more and segue into the song to bring it all home. "Great idea," I said. So, Deb and I shared a couple of thoughts with

Are You Thinking What I'm Thinking?
A Patchwork Journey Through My Life... So Far

the actors, and then they performed the scene very well, showing clear progress. Deb hit the button, and the backing track started. Caitlin, playing the wide-eyed southern girl yearning for love, simply stood there and delivered the song to her colleague Craig, whose character was a damaged carnival worker, interested but afraid of being hurt.

Her young voice was deep, rich, steady, and somehow mature. The resonance from her entire being seemed to deliver the melody and the meaning, all supported by full and generous breath. She filled the room with her sound, and when she reached a higher range, it was assured and expansive. Time actually slowed for me as I became engrossed in this moment. I could feel tears in my eyes; I knew we were only in a small rehearsal room somewhere in Melbourne, and that this moment was fleeting, and we would all go home shortly. Yet, I was genuinely moved and somehow humbled by it all.

When the song finished, Deb looked at me and smiled. "Oh my goodness," or something similar, fell out of my mouth. I thanked Caitlin (and Craig) and took a moment to regroup. Deb and I discussed the day, and then I headed to my car.

On the drive home, I reflected on the day and on that moment so long ago in Top Tote when the wonderful Nick Enright had tears in his eyes. A small moment in a rehearsal room. I know I will never forget this small moment either, small and profound all at once. Art can most certainly sneak up on us. Good luck to Caitlin, Craig, Deb, and to all of us.

And RIP dear Nick.

Director of MOPAC 2021

Are You Thinking What I'm Thinking? A Patchwork Journey Through My Life... So Far

Yamaha 360cc enduro.

It went like a rocket. This was the bike I took away on legendary trail riding weekends up to the Victorian High Country at Woods Point with many Elthamites. Tearing along the fire trails making horrid amounts of noise to challenge the wildlife and any peace seeking bushwalkers. At night there were raging bonfires, endless beers and joints, much frivolity and laughter. Mid to late 70s I guess.

Yamaha RT2 360cc Enduro

Bill Hunter

I guess I first saw Billy on an episode of *Homicide* or *Division 4* when I was a child, though I can't quite recall the exact moment. My earliest clear memory of him, however, is from the 1978 classic Australian film *Newsfront*. His outstanding portrayal of the laconic, slightly weary camera operator for Cinetone News, Len Maguire, earned him the Australian Film Institute's Best Actor award that year. The film was produced by David Elfick and directed by Phil Noyce, featuring an exceptional cast including Gerard Kennedy, Wendy Hughes, Chris Haywood, and Angela Punch-McGregor, who took home the Best Supporting Actress award that year. *Newsfront* swept the awards, winning Best Film, Best Director, Production Design, Costume Design, Original Screenplay, and Best Editing. It remains a towering achievement in Australian cinema, a spellbinding, historically

Are You Thinking What I'm Thinking?
A Patchwork Journey Through My Life... So Far

grounded, socially aware, character-driven picture that masterfully balances all these elements.

Newsfront is a must-watch for anyone interested in Australian history and cinema, offering a vivid glimpse into 1950s Australia while standing as a powerful testament to the rise of Australian filmmaking in the late 1970s. Over the course of my career, I've been fortunate enough to work with several of the cast and crew involved in its making.

As the years went by, I continued to see Billy in brilliant films such as *Strictly Ballroom*, *Muriel's Wedding*, and Peter Weir's masterpiece, Gallipoli. I then had the opportunity to work with him on *The Adventures of Priscilla, Queen of the Desert*. I remember spending an entire night with him during the filming of the Drive-In scene. We sat in the caravan for hours, sharing stories about our work over the years, families, politics, films, and acting. It was a genuine pleasure to simply hang out and chat with such a terrific fellow.

We talked about love and relationships, topics of profound importance. It's vital to be able to speak openly about love: what it means, what it costs, how it can be gained or lost, ruined or resurrected. We discussed how it feels internally, what we do within it, and how we might be devoted or detached. Billy explained that he was currently in a relationship, but he wondered whether he'd ever truly experienced love in the way we were discussing. He said he had perhaps only been in love once, and that in his view, that was enough. Despite being married three times, he seemed to suggest that this one love might have been the real deal. I didn't want to press him too hard as he spoke, despite the deep romanticism and poignancy of his story.

In 1959, the American post-apocalyptic science fiction drama *On the Beach* was being shot in Australia. Billy had been a champion swimmer in his youth, holding the world record for the 100 yards freestyle for about ten minutes, until it was broken in the next heat. He qualified for the Australian swimming team at the 1956 Melbourne Olympics but was unable to compete due to a bout of meningitis. It

Are You Thinking What I'm Thinking? A Patchwork Journey Through My Life... So Far

was on this film that he landed job of stand-in swimmer, pounding out strong strokes across Sydney Harbour in place of Gregory Peck. That experience ultimately inspired him to explore acting further, serving as a springboard for his career.

Imagine Billy, tanned and handsome, standing on the Woolloomooloo wharf on a warm Sydney afternoon. The setting sun cast a vivid, golden light over the moored battleship for the shoot. Suddenly, a door on the second level swings open, and a vision appears, one of the most beautiful women he'd ever seen. She steps out and leans on the railing, her presence striking. From about 50 yards away, their gaze meets. Her remarkable deep brown eyes lock onto his baby blues... They exchange smiles. She's wearing a bright red, firm-waisted summer dress, her short, dark hair tousled and lively. Her smile is warm and full, radiating confidence and charm.

She gracefully makes her way down the gangway, heading straight for Billy to introduce herself. "Hello, I'm Ava Gardner."

"G'day Ava, I'm Bill," he replies.

I don't know what unfolded in the days or weeks that followed, but I do know that tears welled in Billy's eyes as he gently recounted that time. He didn't say it, but I think our man had fallen in love with this extraordinary, exotic woman. It's rare and precious, and maybe it only needs to happen once in a lifetime.

He; handsome, earthy and charming. She; so exotic, with breathtaking beauty. His tone was subtle, respectful and reverent in the telling of this beautiful story. Bill had a lovely voice, and his turn of phrase was delightful.

Are You Thinking What I'm Thinking?
A Patchwork Journey Through My Life… So Far

Ava Gardner

A couple of years later, my good mate Alex Morcos and I, after meeting on *Sniper* in 1992, were in the process of making our short film *The Seedling*. We approached Billy to see if he'd be willing to be part of it. Without hesitation, he agreed to participate in a brief but pivotal scene. The scene involved a 'colourful racing identity' in a luxurious five-star hotel room. We managed to secure a room at the Intercontinental Hotel on Macquarie Street, Sydney, to shoot the scene.

Bill was, as always, dependable, straightforward, minimalist in approach, and a pleasure to work with. I directed the scene where the wild, lead character, played by Alex, a troubled, stumbling, somewhat immature man with delusions of grandeur, finds himself in the opulent bathroom of room 1645, madly consuming an illegal substance. All Billy had to do was simply observe him… the camera capturing his reaction, his subtle expressions. Billy exemplified the art of being simple and truthful in acting, and that's exactly what he brought to this small but significant moment in our film.

Once we had locked off the picture, Alex and I submitted it to film festivals around the world. Several months later, in early 1995, we received the exciting news: we had placed either first, second, or third in the short comedy section at the Houston International Film Festival. I'd heard that both Quentin Tarantino and Steven Spielberg had at

Are You Thinking What I'm Thinking? A Patchwork Journey Through My Life... So Far

some point won this award for their short films, though I've never fact checked that, just in case it's not true! We were over the moon with pride and excitement.

Alex immediately told me he was planning to attend the awards ceremony in Houston, Texas, in May 1995. I was disappointed I couldn't afford to go at that time; it felt crucial to be there, to share the moment, but finances didn't allow. Around this period, Billy and I found ourselves on the set of an ABC series, whose name escapes me at the moment. I told him about the nomination The Seedling had been given, and that Alex would be waving the flag for us. But I wouldn't be there in person due to lack of funds.

Billy then said, 'You're going. Meet me at the Tea Gardens', a Bondi Junction watering hole Billy often visited, 'on Tuesday at 5.' So, I did. He bought me a beer, congratulated me on the nomination, and very subtly slipped $5,000 in cash into my pocket. 'Pay me back when you can. You need to be there,' he said with a knowing smile. That's how I found myself on a plane to Houston.

The film went on to win the Best Short Film award. It was an incredible moment. Alex and I met numerous industry people, making valuable connections along the way. I secured a promissory note from some talented Canadian producers, who expressed interest in co-producing a project with me. Together with the highly energised and talented Nick Holland, I had worked to develop and hopefully shoot a musical feature called *Goddess*, which Nick had written.

An initial budget of $300,000 CAD was available through the Canadians, enough to kickstart the project, perhaps a quarter of the total budget at the time. The Canadian team preferred to shoot in Canada, which would open the door to further funding from the Canadian Tourist Bureau. We dedicated ourselves to making the co-production happen, but, like many great film ideas, it eventually ran out of legs. Despite the effort, solid funding was never fully secured.

After this whirlwind two-week trip to Texas and Los Angeles, I returned to Sydney with a renewed sense of purpose. I was now more

Are You Thinking What I'm Thinking?
A Patchwork Journey Through My Life... So Far

certain than ever that my energy and passion would be directed towards telling stories through film, being a filmmaker.

A week after returning, I was fortunate enough to receive a reasonably handsome residual cheque from *Bananas*, a rare occurrence during those years. I called Billy and arranged to meet him again at the Tea Gardens. I bought him a beer and slipped the $5,000 cash into his pocket, grinning from ear to ear. I thanked him profusely for both his work on *The Seedling* and his extraordinary generosity with the loan.

What a gentleman.

My good friends regularly hopped in for a drink at Campbells Creek.

The last time I saw Billy was only a few months before he passed away. I was living in my rough little rental on the 100 acres in Campbells Creek, just me and my good friends, the kangaroos. On that day, I stopped at the Malmsbury hotel drive-through to grab a traveller for the final fifteen minutes of the journey back to my shack. Waiting for the young bloke serving to notice me, I happened to glance through the window into the Public Bar. That's when I saw Billy sitting there. Our eyes met across the room, and he signalled for me to come in.

So, I did. We shared a single beer together and chatted about work, a little about our lives, and life in general. I didn't know at the time that he was unwell, but he knew. As we talked, he looked at me steadily

Are You Thinking What I'm Thinking? A Patchwork Journey Through My Life… So Far

and said, "When I go, Kenny, someone's got to play my roles." He paused, then added with a gentle smile, "Maybe it should be you!"

"Oh mate, that'd be an honour. I'd love to," I replied, feeling a mixture of humility and gratitude.

We laughed, shared a hearty goodbye, and he even came outside to wave me off, knowing, perhaps, that it would probably be the last time. That quiet moment in that small country pub, sharing a last beer with Billy, remains etched in my memory. It was a profound moment. A sacred farewell. The last beer.

Billy was a giant of a man in Australian cinema, a true gentleman, full of respect and support for me throughout the years. He must have forgotten to tell the casting people that he was passing the baton to me for the roles of Billy Hunter. The phone never rang with offers for roles like Frank McGuire, or the brilliant officer in *Gallipoli*, or the crusty, damaged cop O'Rourke in *Scales of Justice*, or Rex Connor in *The Dismissal*.

But, of course, there's no replacing Billy. They broke the mould. RIP mate.

Bill Hunter

Are You Thinking What I'm Thinking?
A Patchwork Journey Through My Life... So Far

Reservoir, a high board, Miss Vagg, Research and... Where actually is my sister?

My father's service to our country rendered him eligible for what was known as a 'war service loan' from the Government. From this, an ex-serviceman (in those days, invariably men) could draw funds and subsequently purchase a home at a reasonably low interest rate. It was the very least we could do as a nation for those who had sacrificed so much for us.

We were living at 72A Summerhill Road, Reservoir – pronounced "Rezervore" – for as long as I can recall, dating back to the early 1960s. When I say 'we', I mean Mum, Dad, and the three boys. The firstborn, our sister Jane, was residing with my mother's mother, Nan, and her steadfast, quiet husband, Pa, in Brunswick. Why did my sister not live with us?

Identical to our home at 72a Summerhill Rd Reservoir

If, as one theory suggests, Jane was some sort of 'peace offering' to Nan and Pa – a consequence of my Mum finally extricating herself from Nan's manipulative domination and then, heaven forbid, marrying beneath her – the glaring question is this: why couldn't Dad find it within himself to stand up to these women for the fundamental right of his firstborn, his wonderful daughter, to be part of our family? If the sheer power of these complex, dominating women was simply too overwhelming, shrivelling him... then I can only say, 'poor fella,

Are You Thinking What I'm Thinking? A Patchwork Journey Through My Life… So Far

our Dad'. You fought for your country, you strived to rise above poverty, you became a fantastic sportsman and an honourable, hardworking father. Yet, the pain inflicted on your daughter and the resulting negative complexities that forever cast a shadow over your sons and the family were so profound. It must have been an immense burden for you to bear. The impact of this event was developmentally and emotionally quite catastrophic for us all – including you.

You did the best you could, dear man… we all do. I know this was by far the heaviest load you ever carried. Our role as fathers is to protect our children. The protection you were able to offer was the best you could manage, but…

And then, at this point, I must be honest. Forty-three years later, my own failure to protect my children meant I was guilty of the very same thing. In a different era, in a different manner, but the same thing nonetheless. I walked out on my family. I failed to protect my children. Fact. I've done my absolute best since then, but… We are, all of us, imperfect beings.

The exclusion of my sister from our home was, and continues to be, a massive wedge driven into the health, well-being, and trust within our family. The elephant in our lives. The firstborn and only daughter, Jane, was left with Nan and Pa in Brunswick when she was three or four. My sister once asked me rhetorically, 'what did I do when I was three?'

There was another unanswerable question in my life that was posed multiple times… a question my mother first asked me when I was very young, 'what's to become of us, Kenny?' It sounds innocuous enough. But I wonder what I actually made of that question; it felt profound and sombre when she asked it. What effect did the asking of this unanswerable question have on me as a child? What's to become of us? I didn't perceive it as a rhetorical question. It landed as a question to which I might have, or she was actually seeking, an answer. When I reflect on that question now, I see and hear it as rather a frightening thing. Was I supposed to be afraid? Was I meant to have some sort of

Are You Thinking What I'm Thinking?
A Patchwork Journey Through My Life... So Far

philosophical or experiential insight to initiate a deeper conversation? How the bloody hell would I know? I'm a kid! The mixed messages given by my complex mother made it impossible to feel in any way emotionally secure with her. She bounced around like a pinball machine in my life. Expect quiet understanding? You get fury. Expect compassion and empathy? You get cold, practical ambivalence. Expect love? She forgets your name. Expect anger? You get tears of love. She was an unfathomable multitude. From a loving perspective, I did not feel safe with her from a very young age; even though she sometimes appeared to be overflowing with love.

My dear sister was forced to somehow navigate this banishment. The cruel Nan lied to her, saying Mum and Dad didn't want her to live with us, and Nan also lied to Mother, saying Jane didn't want to come live with us. If I felt uncertain of my mother's love and attachment, scared of her mood swings and her domination of my father, then what must have been happening to my sister? Banished. No bloody wonder she carried a sack full of abandonment and anger on her back. What an amazing journey she has made to get to where she is in life. I respect and admire her so much.

My sister with 'her captor' as she described Nan. The damaged pic is not surprising

Are You Thinking What I'm Thinking? A Patchwork Journey Through My Life... So Far

And... My mother worked incredibly hard. She held down a full-time job as a nurse's aide at Mont Park Mental Hospital, *and* a full-time job managing just about everything at home in Research. It's no wonder her reliance on alcohol grew over the years. She was working herself to the bone, all while battling her own consuming behavioural issues. And Dad worked equally hard. For fifteen years, he juggled *three* jobs – I'm not exaggerating. He was a milkman, first at West Heidelberg Dairy, and then for many years at Eltham Dairy (working from midnight until 6:30 am). He was a trained hairdresser and for years cut hair at Mont Park Mental Hospital (as it was called). He later worked on the phones there. His weekend job involved shovelling 'chook shit' into bags for fertiliser at Brinkotter's Chook farm, with senior constable Arthur Trayner from Eltham Police and some other bloke. Both Mum and Dad worked bloody hard for a very long time.

They managed to secure the loan. They bought a small plot of land at number 7 Valley Road, Research; a small town with a shop, post office, butcher, and a fish and chip shop, situated three miles from Eltham on the Panton Hill Road. I loathed the place when we first visited. It was stinking hot, dry, and full of trees, ants, and flies. And it was teeming with highly venomous Tiger Snakes, Brown Snakes, and Yellow-bellied Black Snakes – loads of them. They hung around the creek just down from our property, hunting for food. I absolutely dreaded the thought of living there. But live there we did. It was 1966, the year Australia converted from pounds, shillings, and pence to dollars and cents. I was nine years old. I remember being collected from Preston Northeast Primary School for the journey to Research, for our first night there. I was desperately sad to leave my friends, whom I'd worked so hard to try and get to like me. I was crying and refusing to get into the car. *Slam!* The passenger door closed on my finger. Perfect... Now I had a legitimate reason to cry for the entire journey to our new nightmare, and really ram home to my cruel parents the punishment they were inflicting upon me. Our new home was a small, three-bedroom, one-bathroom brick veneer, built into the sloping

Are You Thinking What I'm Thinking?
A Patchwork Journey Through My Life... So Far

block about 200 metres from the main road, where the shops and the bus stop were located.

We were now living amongst those dreaded snakes, noisy Bellbirds, and warbling Magpies. But by far the most worrying and consuming element was navigating the extremely unhealthy dynamic between my mother and father. When I reflect on their relationship, I realise I never once heard them have what I'd consider a normal, balanced conversation. Their connection was dominated by misunderstanding, a lack of listening and empathy, victimhood and defensiveness from my father, versus domination and quite fierce control by my mother. They argued and yelled so often; it was awful to be around. They'd had a huge row some years before, when we were living in Reservoir. It was frightening. Mum hit Dad, and he shook his fist so close to her face. He never struck her, but he had a wild temper and was as strong as an ox. They lined us three boys up on the couch and asked us, one by one, who we wanted to live with: Mum or Dad? We were hysterical with crying and fear. I found myself either disappearing to another place, physically or mentally, or – perhaps it was middle-child syndrome – trying to intervene, to be the umpire, appealing for calm and understanding, performing for them to distract from the shocking disconnect they presented. "Look at me! I'm acting! Look at me, I'm being edgy and kooky and funny. Look at me, I'm good at footy, at sport, at music, at almost everything I have a go at!!! Stop fighting!!! Please stop fighting!" This performing business was not new to me. I had been performing since I was tiny. Maybe the need for it was multi-faceted: genetic? A natural proclivity? A controlling behaviour, developed by an insecure little boy to try and make people (especially my mother) like me? To show my parents I was worth keeping in the home? "They banished your sister for some unknown reason, remember, kiddo... You might be next! Keep dancing, mate; maybe it'll work!"

There were a few illnesses. Apparently, I was on death's door with the aforementioned viral meningitis when I was six. I was hospitalised for six weeks in the Austin. They were very worried about me. Nobody

Are You Thinking What I'm Thinking? A Patchwork Journey Through My Life... So Far

was allowed to visit for a while. My parents had to speak to me through the blue curtain. They asked me what I wanted; anything at all, they would get it for me. I asked for a clock. Apparently, the passing of time has always been of interest to me. They brought me a Flintstones clock, which I loved. I also fell in love with the nurse. I felt so safe with her. Miss Vagg, the sister of VFL footballer, Barrie – a valuable, six-foot Premiership-winning half-forward for the Melbourne Football Club in the 1960s. Miss Vagg arranged for me to be given a letterhead page from Melbourne, with the signature of every senior player. Barrie was number 32. There were names like Ron Barassi, Hassa Mann, Brian Dixon, Bluey Adams, and others on the page. Their signature, and always their number right next to it. An amazing gift for a sick kid who loved footy. It's not surprising I loved her.

I had six lumbar punctures over that period. A long needle is inserted into the spinal cord to extract cerebrospinal fluid for diagnosis – extremely painful. I remember tears in Miss Vagg's eyes as she held my hand. Meningitis can result in permanent damage or death. The brain's covering, the meninges, is inflamed, either virally (the worst kind, because medication was ineffective, *then* anyway) and can be catastrophic for the patient. After I was released from hospital, everything I tried to write was backwards, in mirror image. As you already know, dear reader, I wrote Miss Vagg a card in this way. I cried a lot, missing her. Nurses are angels, according to that little boy. This truth, like so many others, would be challenged later in life. "Never meet your idols!" I don't know who said that, but it's true. One day, I felt sick at Research Primary. The school phoned my mother, who was at home, asleep. She and Dad were working night shifts at that time – two nights on, two nights off – at Larundel and Mont Park Mental Hospitals. Mum was the nursing aide, and Dad was on the switchboard... "Larundel Hospital," he'd say, in his lovely voice. Anyway, my brother John was allowed to give me a 'dink' home from school on his pushbike, down the hill to Ingrams Road, and then along the track to our house. Going down the Main Road hill, I was balanced on the crossbar of his red bike. I absentmindedly stuck the heel of my school shoe into the spokes of the front wheel. We went arse over head onto the bitumen. Luckily, there were hardly any cars about in those days, so we could lie there bleeding for a bit before dragging the bike off the road, and then carrying it, in a limping fashion, down the hill, across the creek, up the Pocock's driveway, over the fence, and into our place.

Flashback to Reservoir pool High Diving board... Summer, circa 1964.

I was seven. It was a bloody hot day in Melbourne. We had long, hot summers back then – every year. The weather seemed to be more stable in those days.

'Don't go on the high diving board!', Mum had insisted. Mrs Earle was looking after us boys, and we were allowed to walk from the Earles' place to the local pool. And that's exactly what we did. No adult accompanied us; supervision wasn't quite as prevalent then.

The pool was packed, and the high diving board was beckoning. It was my first time. My God, it was a long way up! I think I managed three successful jumps, and, inevitably, I got a bit cocky on the fourth. I remember being soaking wet, all I recall is the blue speedos of the boy in front. I must've slipped.

The next thing I knew, I had a hazy, cinematic-style awakening to that familiar shot: looking up from the ground, a victim's-eye view of a circle of faces peering down at me, with a bright blue sky and the sun behind them. I saw some blood next to me and started crying. My chin really hurt. Then, one of the pool attendants picked me up. He was striding briskly towards the first-aid room, and I heard him urgently bark to someone, 'Get an ambulance! Call PANCH Hospital!' I feebly garbled, 'Idonwannagotohoshpital!' I may have slipped unconscious again because the next thing I recall is being on the first-aid bench. They were asking me who I was with. 'My bruvver.' 'What's his name?' 'John Radley…'

Are You Thinking What I'm Thinking? A Patchwork Journey Through My Life... So Far

Then, I heard over the PA system, 'John Radley, please come to the first-aid room.' He arrived, looking sheepish and a bit annoyed at me. Just then, the ambulance crew came in. They were asking for my name and details, and then they asked my brother John, 'Do you want to come with your brother to the hospital?' 'No,' he said. 'COMEWIFFME!!!' I pleaded. He did, thank goodness.

I remember feeling important as they wheeled the gurney out to the old grey Dodge ambulance – all the people looking at me. They loaded me in, with John sitting up front, like Jacky, in the middle of the bench seat. No lights or sirens, just a kid with a very sore chin. At the hospital, they gave me some orange drink and told me to count to ten. I reckon I made it to six. I woke up with a big bandage on my chin. The nurse asked me if I thought I could walk. I said yes, got up out of the treatment chair, and immediately fell over. They took me to a ward.

Later, I heard my parents fussing as they entered the ward, and I started up again with the tears. 'Kenny, what's wrong?', my mother asked. 'You're going to be mad at me for going off the high board...' 'Oh, my boy,' she said. 'No, we're just happy that you're alright,' as she held me tight. I trusted her when she held me tight.

The lesson I learned through all this? Always make sure there are three points of contact when climbing... I still have the scar, of course.

Austin Hospital 1960s

The high board 1960s

Are You Thinking What I'm Thinking?
A Patchwork Journey Through My Life... So Far

1969 Bushfires

The summers used to be hot. The summer of '68/'69 was one of 'em. January 8th, 1969 (I was 11) was a Total Fire Ban Day across Victoria. Temperatures of 100 degrees Fahrenheit (38 degrees Celsius) and wicked northerly winds of 100kph whipped across the state. 230 fires broke out that day. A fast-moving grass fire engulfed the Melbourne/Geelong expressway near Lara, killing 17 people who left their cars and tried to run from the fire. Six more people, who stayed with their cars, actually survived. (This event was a catalyst in changing guidelines; recommending people are safer staying with their vehicles when a fire is upon them.) In total, 23 people died, 100 were injured, and 230 homes and 21 buildings were destroyed. Our Shire of Diamond Valley was one of the worst affected that day. In our town of Research, 37 houses were burned down. The wailing fire siren atop Orb Gibson's butcher shop, just over the creek on Main Road, was working overtime that day.

We were constantly tuned in to ABC radio for updates on the movement of the fires. In such strong wind and these extremely hot, dry conditions, things happened very fast. We guessed there would be an evacuation call at some point, as the whole of Diamond Valley Shire was under immediate threat. Mum packed a couple of bags with clothes and put all the photographs and any small mementos in the boot of the car. Among them was the most determined trophy I had been awarded for the Greensborough Maroons under 13s team that year. I had not yet made the change to Eltham Panthers football club. Football was my dream as a kid. Motorbikes, girls, surfing and rock 'n' roll were still a couple of years away.

The smoke got thicker. My father suffered from vertigo; he couldn't climb ladders or stairs, and even winding mountain roads got to him. So, Mum and Dad told my brother Peter and me to climb onto the roofs of both our house and the old weatherboard across the road. The McClarens owned it, I think. They weren't home. We stuffed rags into

Are You Thinking What I'm Thinking? A Patchwork Journey Through My Life… So Far

the downpipes of the houses, then filled the guttering with water, a tiny effort against the oncoming inferno.

The garden hose was running at less than one quarter of its usual pressure due to massive water use in the Shire. Meanwhile, Dad had a bucket, and he was scooping water out of our small, above-ground pool in the backyard at the end of the house, heaving it onto the roof like a machine. He was strong and fit and had just turned 42 years of age. The water was flying through the air as if it was being pumped from a fire hydrant. Here was a man using every cell in his body to save the family home. Somehow, he was bouncing water off the chimney at the very back of the house.

Things were getting very worrying now. We did the final loading of the car. We could hear the roar of the fire up and just over the hill. Then, the police car came down, single blue light twirling. With a megaphone, they were ordering us to evacuate immediately. We did. I took a black and white photo of the lower paddock after we had closed all the windows and I had the dog under my arm (the cat had bolted hours ago). As we moved quickly to the car, I asked Dad if we were insured. 'Yes, mate,' came the reply. I don't think I knew what insurance was, only that you're supposed to have some. I was the last to get into the white, '67 Falcon we owned at that point. Just as I was about to climb into the fully loaded back seat, I saw through the smoke a Country Fire Authority truck, red light spinning, racing up Story Avenue towards Research Park, just up the hill from our place. There were maybe six volunteer firefighters on the back, all wearing the knapsack manual pumps that were used in those days. They had heavy gloves and goggles on (the smoke destroys eyes and vision). They wore heavy white masks, soaked in water, and full coverage of uniform to try to minimise radiated heat on a huge scale. These men, all volunteers, were racing towards Armageddon. I could just make out the name on the truck: Coldstream. These men from Coldstream were going to try to protect our houses. We fled to Research shops through the thickest smoke.

Are You Thinking What I'm Thinking?
A Patchwork Journey Through My Life... So Far

There were hundreds of people there. The shopkeepers were giving free cold drinks to everyone. A disaster will bring a community together. We were as one now, and all we could do was wait.

The all-clear was given about two hours later. There were police and fire trucks everywhere. People slowly made their way back to their homes, fingers crossed. Thirty-seven homes gone in Research; ours was somehow still standing, as were all the homes in our little pocket of Valley Road. The Coldstream truck was still up there, slowly traversing Research Park, putting out spot fires. The fire had come within 30 metres of our place. The Coldstream men had saved our homes. It was an extraordinary effort. One truck, six men. We went inside and kept the car loaded in case there was a wind change (a south-westerly change was due at some point). We all put on woollen jumpers, jeans, and the heaviest footwear we could find, then went off in small groups with broomsticks and knapsacks. The broomsticks had heavy rags attached, soaked in water. If you slap them down onto a spot fire, it will put that fire out. Tree stumps and logs were burning. There was still undergrowth that could rekindle, so our job was to contain little spot fires all around the area. We stayed out until late that night doing this.

We were very lucky. The next morning, we gathered in the backyard. The bucket was still sitting next to the two-thirds-filled pool. Dad had emptied a couple of thousand litres, I guess, in his frenzy. We talked about how far he was throwing the water yesterday. 'Have a go now, Dad.' He did. He tried twice. He seriously could not even reach the house with his efforts. Yesterday, he was bouncing water off the bloody chimney at the other end! He was exhausted, and we all were.

There was a lot of sadness and plenty of support being offered over the next few weeks in our community. We had John Dearing, the youngest of the three Dearing boys, stay with us for two weeks, as their home had gone. I recall a nice new one being constructed there over the next few months. White bricks, shiny roof, lovely windows. I guess they had insurance.

Are You Thinking What I'm Thinking? A Patchwork Journey Through My Life... So Far

1969 bushfires – the pic I took as we evacuated

VW Superbug 1600... and a call from Sydney.

Can't remember the cost, or even the year. I just loved this thing. European sports car. I'd had extractors put on it, so yes, definitely a Euro sports unit. Around this time, I joined Sneak Preview, so I was driving all over Melbourne and the outer suburban reaches for three to five gigs a week, as well as working (not well) every day on the tools – sometimes carpentry, sometimes on the shovel, barrow, and mixer as a brickie's labourer. It was so much driving! In the Christmas of 1981, while I had this little beauty of a car, I also auditioned for NIDA. The National Institute of Dramatic Art. THE place to study acting at that time. I did the first audition... and just fell instantly in love with the vibe and the possibility of this life-changing electrical storm building

Are You Thinking What I'm Thinking?
A Patchwork Journey Through My Life... So Far

in front of me. Then, I was lucky enough to get a call back for the second day. An intense day of movement, improvisation, exercises, acting. This day totally confirmed for me where I wanted to be. I had found my people.

Then, a couple of weeks later, the phone rang at my girlfriend Tricia's place in Yallambie, Melbourne. I was down the road – teaching young Shane, her three-year-old boy, to ride a bike, if my memory serves me correctly. Trish came out onto the stoop that ran down from her front door. And her voice, quivering with trepidation, announced, 'Ken, it's NIDA on the phone!' I jogged up the hill, strode up the stoop. I saw the tears on her face as I eased past her through the front door... picked up the phone... 'Hello?' I have not had a more life-changing two minutes in all my life. They had called to offer me a place to join the 1982 cohort and engage in full-time study at the premier acting college in Australia. Almost every Aussie actor I admired had been through this place. A crux moment, yes. Another one.

VW Superbug

Flying to various cities with Nicholas for the open days.

We'd always have a refreshing G&T on the flight, make sure we signed fan cards for the cabin crew and be suitably humble and charming all the way. I recall entering a big bar, eatery place in Darwin with Nicholas, beautiful sticky, warm evening... we just stood there, taking

Are You Thinking What I'm Thinking? A Patchwork Journey Through My Life... So Far

it in. he says to me, 'none of these people have any idea who we are.' So funny. He used to say it was like he'd signed a Faustian deal of some sort. Yes, you can be famous... but there's a catch.

One of the actors somehow holding it all together as he waits for lunch to be called.

John Jarratt & Fields of Fire

I first met this straight-talkin' Queenslander on *Dark Age*, shot in and around Cairns in the mid-1980s. He was playing the lead, along with Nikki Coghill. I played an offsider to Max Phipps's slightly lunatic croc hunter. This was my first time working with Andrew Lesnie, the great cinematographer, who won the Academy Award for *Lord of The Rings* in 2002. He was a delight! But Johnny Jarratt!... he taught me heaps – not so much on *Dark Age*, as we had no scenes together, but later, on *Fields of Fire* (Channel 9/Palm Beach Pictures Mini-Series), shot in 1986 around Yamba on the NSW northern coast we worked together heaps! A wonderful experience in a great location, working with some fine actors. I played Dave, one of the cane cutters in 'Tiny's gang'. It was set in 1938. Plenty of blokes, plenty of Aussie dialogue, plenty of trying to navigate your way around busy scenes with many cast members positioning themselves both for the story, and also to be seen...

Johnny taught me, among many things, 'Look after yourself, mate. Make sure the camera can see you. What's the point of you doing all this bloody NIDA acting if no one sees it?' And... 'Mumble on the wide

Are You Thinking What I'm Thinking?
A Patchwork Journey Through My Life... So Far

shot, Kenny. That way, the editor will be forced to use your close-up in the cutting room. If not, at a minimum, you'll get an ADR (automatic dialogue replacement) day.' So, Johnny taught me lots of the mechanics of film acting. The practicalities of making your contribution worthwhile when you're one of many. When you're in the troop of soldiers, the six or seven cops at an incident. Johnny was brilliant at inventing little things that kept him busy, kept him shootable. All valuable stuff – finding the balance between serving the story, but making sure your contribution as a professional is noticed.

It's actually so much easier playing larger parts. You know that the camera will be switched to you because it has to for the progression of the story. They will cover your dialogue and action because it has to be covered. You don't have to invent 'interesting' stuff to validate the presence of your character. It's tricky... small parts are really tricky – and I've done heaps of them. Thirty feature films, at least 60 TV appearances over a 40-year career. So yeah, I've played many 'small, but pivotal' roles. Johnny helped me recognise and develop a whole lot of useful tools in these areas. JJ became a good mate for many years.

The late, excellent, Harold Hopkins, fabulous Kris McQuade, myself, Johnny Jarratt, my great friend Todd Boyce, Jack Mayers, The late Ollie Hall, a wonderful man. And the ever-laconic Bill Young as Lofty in the Palm Beach Pictures/Channel 9 series Fields of Fire. 1986. One of the great experiences of my career.

Are You Thinking What I'm Thinking? A Patchwork Journey Through My Life... So Far

Jacko, Tiny, Dave and two angel nurses. The World War 2 section of Fields of Fire.

The Kombi

Kenny had one, orange. His dad, Sid, had one also; his was dark blue. Both were the older style Kombis with twin windshields and two barn doors that swung outwards from the van. I think I was 15 when I met the late Kenneth John Hughes. Kenneth, Kenny, Limey, K1, as I called him in later years. I had so many adventures with him that it deserves a chapter, a book, an anthology! He was four or five years older than me. I felt instantly close to Kenny the moment I met him. He was quiet, thoughtful, handsome, and so clever at fixing things. If cars broke down, and they often did in them days... the good ol's... Kenny would quietly and methodically go about investigating and dealing with the issue. Countless times he got us out of trouble with carburettor complexities, electrical problems, coils, distributors, spark plugs, leads, connections, gearsticks, linkages, bushes, Welsh plugs, and countless other anomalies. He almost never asked for help. With cars or indeed in building. As a matter of course, he would simply find a way to do it by himself. I'll chat more about building in another chapter.

I fell out of Kenny's Kombi.

Are You Thinking What I'm Thinking?
A Patchwork Journey Through My Life... So Far

Once, just outside Eltham, late at night, we were all at a party in a flat (I think a woman called Helen lived there) near where Wattletree Road meets Main Road. The orange Kombi, which was covered in hippy images – flower power, slogans, hand-painted peace symbols, multi-coloured fun images all over it - was parked just up the hill. Right next to it was an open trench. There was no safety webbing or flashing yellow lights to assist the public in keeping themselves safe. Oh no, just a 1500mm deep trench with piles of loose rubble right next to it. I had been drinking; no doubt there was greenery involved, there was always greenery involved! So, I waddled up to the Kombi to get something, who knows what? I slipped and slid on the rubble as I opened the swinging doors. Then I lost balance completely and fell backwards, lengthwise, into the trench. It felt for all the world like I was in a grave. I couldn't move; I was wedged on my back with my arms trapped under me. I squealed for help, but things were pretty quiet back then, probably about 1973. So, no one came to assist me. Every time I tried to wiggle, a huge amount of earth would fall in on me. I was gradually becoming buried. Headline: Drunk idiot eats dirt, then dies! I actually felt like I might die there. After what felt like half an hour, I made a huge effort, using all my wiggle power. I closed my eyes, shut my mouth and somehow rose from certain death. Spitting earth out of my mouth, shaking all the dust and rubble from my ears, I staggered back to the party, burst in dramatically and asked, 'Have you ever felt death creeping up your legs?' Of course, they all laughed at my stupid, dust-covered, drunk face.

I fell out of Sid's Kombi.

One Saturday morning, Kenny was driving Sid's Kombi somewhere near Reservoir or Preston, for some reason. Sid's Kombi had a single bed in the back. It had a wrought-iron, rounded bedhead, sitting up on iron legs, with a nice mattress. Maybe Sid had it in there so he could kip after playing a gig. He played banjo in a trad jazz band. I was lying on my stomach on the bed, yapping away to Kenneth in the front. I can't remember if anyone else was with us. Kenny goes around a right-hand roundabout. These old Kombis didn't handle well at all. No

Are You Thinking What I'm Thinking? A Patchwork Journey Through My Life... So Far

power steering, kind of prehistoric running gear, suspension, and technology, in true VW style of the era. The van body rolled to the left as we rounded the bend. The old wrought-iron bed was pretty precariously positioned and rather top-heavy, with young Radley sprawled lengthwise on it. The bed tilts to the left, then tilts further as Kenny goes deeper into the turn. It all goes past the point of no return; I am clutching at fresh air, trying to find a skyhook to grab on to. Bang! It crunches onto the double opening doors, they crash open, and I tumble out onto the bitumen. The rear wheel misses my head by millimetres. I do a stunt roll, leap up onto the grass verge and start running around in circles. The bed didn't quite fall out of the van. Kenny lurched to a halt. Thank goodness the traffic volume was so much lower in those days (early to mid-70s), so there were no other cars around to be involved in our little moment. 'You ok? You ok?' 'Yes! Jesus, that was close...' We closed up the doors, locked them properly this time. My memory tells me I got in the front then. I don't recall even taking any bark off with my 'pavemental' close encounter. Just another near-death experience. Have you ever felt death rolling past your head?

The Kombi era

I got a $1,300 loan to buy a Kombi minibus. Windows all around. I took the seats out, had some red curtains made (a student once told me red is my fave colour), built a bed in the back, and installed a state-of-the-art Pioneer cassette player with speakers in the front and back, a bull bar, board racks, and a mesh screen to stop rocks from smashing the windscreen, and extractors to give it a little more oomph. I had a wonderful dog called Barney and had begun surfing with some friends down at Phillip Island. Working on the carpentry tools during the week, singing with the band, surfing on the weekend... living the dream. What a life! I was never a good surfer at all! Did a lot of paddling and trying to 'spring' up to my feet. Looking back, I reckon the board was too short for a beginner. A longer board would have given me more stability and let me pick up the swell earlier to gradually increase the skills. But hey, we had so many parties in the back of that Kombi!

Cut to late afternoon Winter, Woolamai Beach, Phillip Island.

A lifesaving moment...

A thoroughly lacklustre surf day, it was. Out there with Whippo, Skin, Greg Stewart, Clemmy Stewart, and my mate Trevor Stewart – a gathering of the Stewart clans! It was a grey, winter's day, and there was absolutely no organisation to the way the surf was presenting itself. It was choppy, with no discernible take-off points and no real place where we could all congregate. Consequently, we were spread out, and at best, we were just hoping for a fleeting little peak where we could manage a take-off, and perhaps, for the better surfers amongst us, a minuscule bottom turn before it all just fizzled out. Really, we were just passing time, paddling about and becoming a tad frustrated. I was particularly cheesed off because, not being blessed with any semblance of surf skills, I was deriving absolutely no pleasure out there. The sun, obscured by the clouds, was not far from setting as the boys all signalled and decided to paddle in and call it a day. I thought I'd hang about for another few minutes to try and at least get to my feet once during the entire session. It didn't happen, though. The light was fading rapidly, so I gave up on catching any sort of wave and began paddling towards the shore. There wasn't even a hint of swell to assist my return, so I simply dug in to paddle my way back. And I paddled, and I paddled... I felt like I wasn't making any progress at all, so I started scratching with more vigour and determination. Still, I didn't seem to be covering any distance whatsoever... mmm, that was odd. The boys had all gone over the sand dune towards the car park, leaving me on my own. I glanced way off to my right, where there was a solitary tree on a hill within sight. The tree hadn't moved, or perhaps it had... a little bit... the wrong way! 'Bugger it,' I said out loud, 'I'm gonna go for it now, this is not right.' I was quite fit and strong at the time, what with surfing and working on the carpentry tools all week,

Are You Thinking What I'm Thinking? A Patchwork Journey Through My Life... So Far

so I had some reserves to put in a real effort. And I did; I gave it absolutely everything I had. For several minutes, I pounded and scratched at that choppy grey water in the very dim light, like a young man gripped by the beginnings of panic. I was getting nowhere. Now I was yelling at the bloody ocean to take me in, ordering the sea to deliver me to where I needed to be! I was on the verge of a full-blown panic attack. Going backwards, actually going further out, not in. I looked up. I could just make out the silhouette of my good friend Trevor Stewart standing on top of the dune with his board under his arm. I sat up on my board, utterly exhausted, and waved my arms in the cross-pattern 'help me' style. Stewy legged it down the beach. He jumped on his board, paddled like a champion out about fifty metres, and gestured with absolute clarity that he wanted me to paddle to my left – along the beach. I did as he indicated, found some more strength, and paddled left as hard as I could. Then, after a while, the blessed relief of a wave crashed over me. I got on the board and paddled towards the shore; another wave hammered me, and now I was getting closer. Then another wave, then another. Now I could walk, pushing the board and gliding the last twenty-five metres or so onto the glorious sand of Woolamai Beach. I needed to sit down for a minute to compose myself. Stewy checked on me, "You alright, Rags?" (my nickname at the time). The rest of the boys were atop the dune now, looking down at us. I sheepishly made my way back to the Kombi in the car park, where Barney greeted me with the unrestrained joy that only your dog can provide. The lads explained that I'd been caught in a rip; I had absolutely no idea what a rip was. But by Jesus, I certainly know what one is now. Surfers often utilise them as express trains to take them out to the back of the break, then they peel off the rip and paddle over to the take-off zone. Knowing about rips is a crucial piece of knowledge for beachgoers in Oz! Stewy saved my life that day – I was in real trouble. I'm eternally grateful to that man. He's an above average plumber as well!

Are You Thinking What I'm Thinking?
A Patchwork Journey Through My Life... So Far

Living the dream

The Diesel

The rhythmic dug-ada-dug-ada of an engine announced its arrival as it pulled up outside the old blacksmith's shop where I was working on a warm, still Tuesday afternoon in Castlemaine. The ceiling was now awaiting its undercoat, the plasterers having completed their work. It was a bright, sunny day, and I was lost in my own world of thoughts and daydreams.

Glancing through the window, I noticed it was a Mercedes van. At the time, I was working on and off for Mainstreet Theatre Company, based in Mount Gambier, South Australia. The van bore a resemblance to the sort that Mark Stratford, the company's business manager, and I had discussed. This type of vehicle would be ideal for the long-haul tour we were planning for the following year. Keen to inspect one of these vans, I ambled outside and stood there, observing it. A bloke hopped out of the driver's side. "How's it run?" I enquired. "Great!" he replied, with a thick American accent. "This baby will cruise at 120 clicks all day long. It's an ex-ambulance. The air conditioning unit in the back there, see that? That's worth twelve thousand dollars on its own."

He had the look of someone who might have been a cowboy in a previous life. Not particularly tall, wearing jeans, a belt, and boots. A touch bow-legged. Friendly enough, though. "It's got a five-cylinder diesel engine, drives like a car," he drawled. "What did you pay for it?" I asked. "Thirty-two thousand dollars. They're worth seventy new,

Are You Thinking What I'm Thinking? A Patchwork Journey Through My Life... So Far

but the ambulance service updates them every two years or 100,000 kays, whichever comes first." I liked the idea of a good, sturdy Merc for the long journey ahead but was considering the amount of space inside. It needed to accommodate the set, lighting and sound equipment, props, personal belongings, and have enough room for a couple of aircraft seats for passengers. "Is there much room inside?" I wondered aloud. The windows were heavily tinted, making it difficult to see in. "Plenty of room," he declared with a flourish as he slid the side door open.

In the middle of the van, a wheelchair was securely fastened to various anchor points. Seated in the wheelchair was a woman. She looked wasted and grey, her hair shaved very short, her head lolling to one side. There was some dribble at the corner of her mouth, and a vacant, faraway expression in her pale blue, staring eyes. Her body was twisted into what appeared to be an extremely uncomfortable position. "That's my wife," he announced. I was somewhat taken aback by the sight of her and couldn't immediately think of what to say. "Hey," I blurted out, intending it to be a benign and non-confrontational "hi, how are you doing?" She didn't acknowledge me or make any sound. She simply sat there with her dribble, blankly staring into the middle distance of the back of the van. "We had a bad road accident in Turkey two years ago. This is her chariot!" he cheerfully explained, before slamming the door shut. "I'll get the number of the bloke who deals in these things for you. He's the most honest car dealer I've ever met!" I stood there, looking at the tinted window, knowing she wasn't looking at me. I felt awkward, unsure of the appropriate way to behave towards her. I wanted to ask if she could hear or understand me, but I sort of froze up. "Nah, I don't have it on me," he shouted. "Here, here's my number, give me a call, and I'll give you this bloke's number."

I thanked him, told him my name, and extended my hand. He shook it vigorously. "Kramer, Jerry Kramer, give me a bell." With that, he hopped in and eased the Merc off down the road, its reliable five-cylinder diesel engine clattering away.

Are You Thinking What I'm Thinking?
A Patchwork Journey Through My Life... So Far

I freshened up my paintbrush, wondering about the roads in Turkey.

Sniper, 1992

Judy Davis & The Detailed Work Of An Expert

The film *Children of The Revolution* (1996), penned and directed by Peter Duncan, provided a memorable experience. I played the pivotal role of Bernard Shaw, while the late, great Marshall Napier, played my brother, Brendan. My scenes with Judy were few, but significant. As I've said, I am rarely swayed or intimidated by fame, celebrity, or reputation. I've worked with heaps of 'big stars' and we are there to work, that's what we do. However, with this person that I had long regarded as a Queen of Australian cinema, it all felt a little different.

Judy arrived with a formidable reputation, whispered to be a rather challenging and somewhat daunting individual to work alongside. For over a decade, I had admired her artistry in countless Australian and international films, absorbing lessons as I honed my own craft and delved into the intricacies of cinema and acting. Consequently, I approached this brief encounter with a keen sense of anticipation. Predictably, I remained quiet and meticulously professional during our initial scene – my character was smashed on the couch, which suited me perfectly. I didn't have to actually do anything! But I could quietly watch the way Judy was working. And I did; a quiet, unwavering assuredness. A calm familiarity, instinctively noting the placement of props, light stands and crew. She had an undeniable air of professional reverence surrounding her; everyone understood that Judy was at work. There are hushed tones and general care and awareness by the

Are You Thinking What I'm Thinking? A Patchwork Journey Through My Life... So Far

crew. She carried an inherent 'star clout,' and rightly so, she's earned it, a brilliant practitioner.

Stars or industry heavyweights are somehow automatically offered this care and consideration when they are on set.

A little more about the dynamics on set: It is actually quite difficult when fellow cast or crew members have little or no regard for the work of the actor. Occasionally, more in the past than these days, there were times some crew members either did not give consideration to, or had no idea of the focus requirement that may be needed to arrange oneself for the forthcoming moment in this scene. They're busy with their stuff. Every department is primarily focussed on their job... it's a film about makeup, it's a scene about costume, or lighting, or props, or the track... they're all doing their thing and will get their butt kicked if they screw up; by the head of department or by the first AD or by the producers. The actor's job is to shut up, wait until 'stand by' is called and be ready for the word 'action.' This is why the type of concentration needed on a film set is quite particular for an actor. You spend sooo much time waiting for all sorts of things to be done. The task is to retain a level of focus that is required for the work. To find a way to be available; physically and mentally for the scene at a moment's notice when you are called to set. So, each actor needs to understand how they need to be, where their mind needs to be, and be ready and able to play the scene 100% correctly when the moment comes. It can be tricky. Personally, I need to sit or be quiet and focussed whilst waiting – I don't like my concentration to be all over the place, I like to be ready to work. Hence, I'm usually a little quiet and removed while on set. Not in Bananas of course, which was controlled, energised mayhem!

Back to Judy... There was a shot where the camera began on her face with some dialogue, then her eyes lower to her shoes; there was some mention or moment to do with shoes. It's just a small thing but I was actually captivated by the precision of her focus and her concentration during the slow crane down, camera following her gaze to the shoes.

Are You Thinking What I'm Thinking?
A Patchwork Journey Through My Life... So Far

Then the shot pushes in on the shoes, then the shoes move, turn and walk away. Just a small moment in the film, I don't even know if it made the final cut. But I watched this consummate professional. In rehearsal trying several little moves on the shoes, different shapes, different timings, different speeds on the departure... all supported by character, all in order to tell the story, all in full awareness of the lighting, shot size, pace. I mean, it's the sort of thing we do as actors... we understand how big the shot is, what speed the move needs to be, what shape the body or indeed the shoe needs to take. This is just part of our skill and expertise, the practising and the detail of our craft. But on that day, it was her doing it, this renowned expert. This multi-award-winning professional was simply doing her thing. And I happened to be observing.

Oh, and she was not at all scary! Professional and quietly respectful. We just worked... that's what we do.

The brilliant Judy Davis in Children of The Revolution. With Sam Neil lurking in the background...

The Night the Angels Came...

A Winter Saturday night. Semi-rural Victoria, Australia, 1977. I had just turned 20. I was feeling excited to sing a few tunes with the band at a fancy-dress party. Our song list was a blend of bluesy rock, soulful numbers, and country tunes, ranging from Al Green's 'Take Me to The River', to 'Nobody Knows You When You're Down and Out' and

Are You Thinking What I'm Thinking? A Patchwork Journey Through My Life... So Far

'Further on Up the Road'. The party was being held at the home of Roy and Sue Webb, whose place sat at the very end of a dirt track – Brown's Lane, I think it was – in Plenty, a remarkably quiet, predominantly rural suburb. I had, in fact, lived in a bungalow behind their property for a spell, just before I rented my first proper home near Coleman's Corner in Main Road, Eltham. That was my inaugural co-habitation with a girlfriend; a steep learning curve for all involved.

Our band had recently welcomed a new, exceptionally talented young guitarist named David Adam. We set up our gear in the lounge room of the Webbs' modest, weatherboard rental, a typical layout for the time: an entrance hall with a bedroom or two leading off it, then the lounge, followed by the kitchen, and finally the back door at the rear of the house.

The place was teeming with people – who could say how many? Crazy costumes abounded, laughter mingled with the clinking of bottles, and copious joints were being passed around. The joint was jumping! As usual at parties in those days there were lots of women in the kitchen – it's just how things were. The women often gathered in the kitchen.

I was pouring my heart into the music when I noticed headlights flashing through the front yard...

Motorcycles. Lots of them.

Then, the whole vibe of the place changed. In walked maybe 10 Hells Angels bikers with their girlfriends. My God they looked ominous. The Sergeant at Arms was a big guy whose name escapes me. He was surrounded by his band of goons. One or two of them were wearing what looked like brand-new colours. We thought later, maybe this was a sort of initiation for them? A rite of passage moment? The Angel chicks had gone to the kitchen. They were clearly casing the joint...

This was long before the Angels had organised themselves into a big money-making enterprise – Money eventually became much more important to the club than simply making an outlaw presence in the world and 'sticking it to the man'.

Are You Thinking What I'm Thinking?
A Patchwork Journey Through My Life... So Far

In our society the God almighty dollar always prevails! In all walks of life.

The Angels were just at the end of their original mission as outlaws making their presence felt as a fringe dwelling law bending operation on the very edge of mainstream society.

After being founded in Fontana, California in 1957 Hells Angels had become a world-wide enterprise with hundreds of clubs and chapters. They were just beginning to flex their international muscles. Eventually they would be regarded by all major international intelligence agencies as an organised crime syndicate... But tonight, they crashed a fancy-dress party full of Hippies in Plenty, Victoria, Australia.

So, the big Sargeant at arms guy positioned himself into a corner, surveying the room. His goons were mingling with the dancers on the floor. Very creepy and unsettling. One of them stepped in between my friends Barry and Linda who were dancing. Baz was and is a peace lover and no fool; he didn't aggravate the guy more than showing an understandable bit of displeasure. Linda didn't like it at all and walked away as the guy was trying to do his unappealing version of dirty dancing with her.

The whole vibe was becoming very heavy.

We stopped playing. One of the Angels came to me and with a chilling calmness said, 'just keep playing and you'll be alright.' The gag I tell people is that I immediately turned to the band and yelled, Springsteen style, 'One, two, three, four!' But I didn't. We were all frozen and very worried. Then I heard a great commotion in the hallway, thumps and bangs and bodies flying everywhere. There was yelling and some screaming from the kitchen. My girlfriend Kerrie came to me holding the side of her face and said, 'one of them just hit me!' I grabbed her and we ducked outside through the commotion. Ross Campbell had been battered in the hallway and looked dreadful – apparently, he had stood up to them. The Angel women had belted some girls in the kitchen; the rookie Angels were dishing out violence to the male party

Are You Thinking What I'm Thinking? A Patchwork Journey Through My Life... So Far

goers. Kerrie and I sneaked out to my white 1966 HD Holden panel van – with a fully worked 192 motor, double barrel carby and 3 on the floor gearbox - It was parked close to the house as I'd carried some band gear in it. We got in, sat low, I started the thing up – regretting the nice burbling note it had. Slipped it into first and began to creep away... an Angel came toward us in the headlights holding an iron rod above his head ready to strike – 'where the fuck are you goin'?... I edged the car backwards and turned off the engine. We slipped down so our heads could not be seen. I surreptitiously locked the doors. We could then hear the sound of glass breaking all the way up the dirt road. The Angels were smashing the headlights of all the cars. There were two women who were trying to escape that had made it to their car. Jan Bebbington and Lyn Bullen – fabulous people trying to find a way out of this nightmare. They hid on the floor of the car as the Angels were smashing not only lights but windows. They must have been absolutely petrified.

Meanwhile two partygoers had slipped away and made a run for the next property to call the police. One was Jono Hurst, a fun-loving legend of the area, who was wearing a huge baby nappy and had moulded a half doll sticking out of his head as a costume for the party. I wonder what the neighbours thought or felt when they opened the door? Had Charles Manson turned up in Plenty on that night?

Having completed their reign of terror on us unsuspecting hippy/tradie/muso/peace lovers The Angles regrouped. They fired up their Harleys and BSA's and Triumphs and Nortons. They also had a car or two with them. Then, they roared off down the road in a cloud of dust leaving us all shocked and terrified. Some partygoers left immediately, quite a few stayed – Roy and Sue were very isolated out there. What if they had gone to get reinforcements? Were they coming back? We should all hang and be in a group. I recall Paul Fox, who was a conscientious objector in the call up for National Service during the American/Australian war on Vietnam, stridently telling us we should gather forces and manpower. We needed weapons to 'go get them!' Nobody agreed, he was so angry. We all stayed there for another 45 minutes to an hour when yet more headlights were coming towards us. Six carloads of Victoria Police arrive an hour after the drama – where is a cop when you need them? Was the cry. They had come from Greensborough and beyond. There was no way they would come to a callout like that without adequate force and weaponry. Police were not armed at that stage, so they would have needed to check out weapons, load them into the boot and gather all sorts of gear together. This was before the days of rapid response groups and military style hardware for cops.

As a non-violent, peace-loving chap, I was shocked and scared over this matter. As was Kerrie. I think we all were. It was terribly frightening. As we walked past the constabulary a cop said to me, 'do you want to make a report?' 'No, that's ok', was my shaky response…

At last, I fired up the HD, easing it off down the road, nervous and shaken. Violence has always had a deep impact on me. Then, I was worried leaving my car outside my rental on Main Road – In full view of Angels who may remember it from the party. I recall thinking, "life will never be the same." This moment had irrevocably altered the fabric of what this area had been.

None of us are safe. Bikers thereafter became the 'tough guy' demographic I was most wary of. Understandable really.

There was a scary dude used to be around Eltham whose name was Doug Scott. I don't know if he was a member of a bikie gang, but he had the look, and the bike. I recall he was dating a rebellious year 12 girl at Eltham High and would come collect her on his big loud bike. She would get astride the bike in her super short school dress just after the last bell, black hair flowing as he roared of down the road, her with arms wrapped around the rebel… there's a song in there somewhere.

'Just wrap your hands 'round my engines…'

The Coffee Shop

A few years before the Angels saga, there was a Sunday evening gathering place for young people at a church in Eltham, known simply

Are You Thinking What I'm Thinking? A Patchwork Journey Through My Life... So Far

as The Coffee Shop. I was probably fourteen or fifteen at the time. There was a piano in the entranceway to the main gathering room. I was enthusiastically banging away on this instrument, belting out 'House of The Rising Sun' with gusto, when *SLAM*... the lid was violently smashed shut. I just managed to get my fingers out in time. It was Doug Scott. He had a look in his eyes that I can only describe as 'mad' – I've only seen such eyes a few times in my life, and his were the very first. I froze.

At this particular time in Eltham, there was also a rather handsome, charismatic, and entrepreneurial young man named Ricky Ozimo. He had been standing with others, listening and watching me bash out the well-known Animals tune on the piano. Immediately after Scott slammed the lid down, Ricky gently lifted it and quietly said, "Keep playing, it sounds good."

I didn't know either of these blokes.

Scott slammed it down again. Ricky calmly raised it. I, of course, was utterly frozen once more! They then grabbed each other, and a flurry of punches and wrestling ensued, sending people scattering in every direction. My brother, John, was nearby. He exclaimed with urgency and some amazement at my rooted-to-the-spot paralysis, "Get out, Ken!" (That was the second time he did that in my life.) So, I bolted. I don't know who won that scrap between those two blokes, but I sincerely hope it was Ricky. I never got the chance to thank him for supporting an emerging young performer!

Bloody biker types, so scary back then.

The Angels...

Are You Thinking What I'm Thinking?
A Patchwork Journey Through My Life... So Far

Honda 100cc Street Bike and Bruce

Bruce was in town... and I'd just picked up a Honda 100cc street bike. Cost me a hundred bucks from Andrew Blaxland, a lovely, 'arty' designer bloke who worked at the ABC in Sydney. At the time, he was married to Antoinette, a fabulous woman and a classmate of mine at NIDA. I bought this unregistered little runaround during my second year at NIDA, just to zip around Paddington and down to Kensington. I didn't have a licence; never have had a bike licence, truth be told. Got two learner permits over the years but never actually took the full test. I offloaded the little beauty after a few months – the tropical rain in Sydney wasn't worth the risk.

I was living at number 39 Sutherland Street, down the less fancy end of Paddington, just down the hill from the Four in Hand Hotel before its massive gentrification. My place was downstairs, a sort of dug-out cave arrangement. It was a funky, rustic little studio with French doors and windows that opened onto a small brick pathway and a tropical garden. A shower and a single-burner gas cooker were about it. All I owned was a wok and two bowls (in case of a visitor...). The bed hung in a corner on four chains, giving it a bit of a sway. There was also a big mirror at the head of the bed. All in all, it was pretty cool. Being the quiet end of Paddington, there were always plenty of birds around and lovely, rich tropical smells in the air – frangipanis and jasmine nearby, and beautiful jacaranda trees with their amazing lavender-coloured blooms for a few weeks each year. It was a lovely place to live, and I spent my entire second year at NIDA there.

Soft and sweet Rhys McConnochie lived in the weatherboard house above me. He taught and directed at NIDA, acted in plays and films, and occasionally had a 'curry Sunday'. He'd invite a guest or two, make a couple or three delicious curries, and ask if I'd like to join them! It felt so sophisticated for me, a rough-headed carpenter type from Melbourne who was lucky enough to get into NIDA. My life had taken a turn for the better in the most welcome ways since coming to Sydney and being involved in the amazing, stimulating world of literature,

Are You Thinking What I'm Thinking? A Patchwork Journey Through My Life… So Far

theatre, poetry, design, and the craft and intense training of acting. Meeting these interesting, quirky, intelligent theatre types, listening to and observing them, was such a great period of growth for me. Rhys is the most wonderful, gentle man with a beautiful voice. He asked me to build him some bookshelves, which I did – all by hand, with no workbenches or power tools. They were actually the prototypes for many that I built over the following years, in all sizes, shapes, and styles, for folks I knew and still know.

With delightful synchronicity, two of my best mates also lived in that little 'love cave' after me over that period: my best mate in the world, dear Greg Stone – a brilliant actor and excellent human being. And my good friend Shane Connor, another great actor – though slightly misguided in his AFL allegiances… some rowdy mob called Port Adelaide.

Springsteen is among us!... 1985… Yes! Somehow, we heard Bruce and the whole E Street Band were up at the Four in Hand playing pool. OMFG, we all gathered and raced up the hill to check it out and maybe even chalk up a cue with the man himself. We missed him by minutes!!! They'd been there all afternoon, having a great, quiet time in a fabulous old-style Sydney pub, racking up a few games and enjoying some quiet beers. The bar staff were all in this great state of frozen-smile euphoria, having been well looked after by the boys and just enjoying the presence of one of the great bands of that era... and as it turns out, every bloody era! We ordered beers and chalked up the cues, knowing that the last people to play on that table, just minutes ago, were the E Street legends. We played a few games of eight-ball in honour and respect... 'Like soldiers on a winter's night with a vow to defend. No retreat, baby, no surrender.' Our great mate Steve Vidler queued all night for tickets for ten of us to go to the show. We took him coffee and croissants for breakfast – what a wonderful effort. The show??? OMG, the show... it was like a religious experience, only better! They began... BEGAN the show with the biggest hit they'd ever had – the powerful anti-war anthem "Born In The USA". It was

Are You Thinking What I'm Thinking?
A Patchwork Journey Through My Life… So Far

absolutely amazing, and it somehow built from there for four hours. You certainly get your money's worth with Bruce.

In a quirk of 'full circle', my upstairs neighbour Rhys got in touch with me a few months ago. He's in his late eighties now and was preparing to go back to New Zealand to live out his twilight years with family. He was in the process of offloading books, posters, and theatre memorabilia gathered over a lifetime. He wanted to know if I'd like to have the bookcases I built for him in 1983 back again. I said, of course, that would be wonderful. So I visited him with the recently resurrected Greg Stone. Yes, Greggy had died a few months before… for 20 minutes, in St Vincents hospital Sydney. The amazing staff brought him back, operated and freshened up his heart so he can grace the stages of Australia for another 50 years! He's made a 100% full recovery. Thank goodness for science and medicine! We had lovely chats with Rhys and loaded the cases up. One of them was too big for me to use, so we passed it on to folks who could! But I do have the other one now, in my humble Elwood rental. The prototype. Chock full of books (some of which I've read) and maybe thirty DVDs, mostly of shows and films I've been in... full circle indeed. And yes, I still have a Blu-ray player for when the WWW collapses!

1979 Honda 100cc Street Bike

Are You Thinking What I'm Thinking? A Patchwork Journey Through My Life… So Far

Warwick Thornton's 'The New Boy', 2023. The trudgen is real, of the period (1940's) Sourced from Adelaide museum by the excellent costume designer, Heather Wallace. I got to drive the fabulous old Morris up a bumpy road… like the good ol' days.

Priscilla… and a gently flowing river of experience

I first clapped eyes on Stephan Elliot, the writer and director of The Adventures of Priscilla, Queen of the Desert, when he was working as an assistant director on a couple of terrific Bill Bennet pictures in the lateish1980s, Jilted and Dear Cardholder. Jilted was shot on what was then known as Fraser Island – a fabulous location. Dear Cardholder was filmed in and around Sydney. Stephan also worked on a great Telemovie I was in called Stock Squad. Stephan; full of snappy humour, a sharp tongue, a quick wit… and a formidable knowledge of film. One Friday on Stock Squad, Stephan was heading into town to hire some VHS videos (remember those?) for the weekend Motel entertainment. he called out to Phil Rich, the First AD, 'what do you want?' 'Nothing under 15 million.' I thought it was a rather cool, direct exchange. Fifteen million and upwards was a pretty serious budget back then, reserved for action flicks and blockbusters. None of your highfalutin German arthouse films mate. Phil wanted some bang for his buck!

We were on location in Gunnedah, New South Wales. *Stock Squad* was a smart little telemovie for, bugger it, I can't recall which network. It starred the excellent Martin Sacks, with whom I struck up a delightful and enduring professional and personal friendship. A truly fabulous man and a great actor. Heart-throb good looks and a charming air of both humour and humility. We laughed and laughed for years until life took us down different paths. I want to share a little something that happened with us in a Phillip Street/Glen Street production about the champion Marty …

Martin Sacks

Marty and I did a bit together on this picture. Our paths crossed again on series two of Fields of Fire, and I did a few episodes of Blue Heelers, where he was a stalwart. We might have even briefly worked together developing an idea for a feature film, I reckon.

But there we were, in the theatre, working on the David Williamson classic, The Club, during July and August of 1987. It was directed by Rob 'Stainless' Steele. On the very first day of rehearsal, Stainless announced in his gravelly, fifty-fags-a-day voice, 'Yeah, we're gonna sit around for a couple of days and read it and do all the bullshit. But this is a comedy, we're going for the laughs…' And we certainly did. Kevin Healy played Jock, the old-time ex-coach; Peter Corbett was Laurie, the current coach; Peter Rowley was a fabulous, high-energy Ted, the President; and Don Chapman played Gerry, the practical money man. I played Danny, the ever-reliable captain who consistently got twenty kicks a game, year in, year out, for twenty years. Marty played Geoff Haywood, the young upstart. A champion with an ego to match, who was being paid more than any player before him.

There's a hilarious scene towards the end of act one, set in the club meeting room – very grand and traditional, with photos of all the old

Are You Thinking What I'm Thinking? A Patchwork Journey Through My Life... So Far

champions adorning the walls. Jock is clumsily trying to forge a matey relationship with Geoff, who takes out his tobacco tin and begins rolling a cigarette...

Jock: 'Ah, you roll your own, do ya?' Geoff: 'Yeah, Jock. Would you like me to roll you one?' Jock: 'Yeah, thanks, Geoff...'

Of course, it wasn't tobacco Geoff was rolling. It was weed. So, the act finishes with a truly hilarious yarn. Geoff is reeling Jock in with an outrageous story from his youth – walking in on the horrendous sight of his father having sex with his legless sister... and how the impact of it has dominated his life ever since, which is why his form has been a bit off lately. Jock is getting progressively more stoned; Geoff is relentless with the story, and the audience is roaring with laughter. Both these actors absolutely nailed this scene; it was side-splittingly funny. Stainless certainly got his laughs!

The substance the actors were smoking was a herbal mixture that smelled remarkably similar to the real deal. Marty asked me to be his designated joint roller in the lead-up to each show. He knew I had the skill, having done it in another show once... so it all went swimmingly for the entire month-long run.

Martin Sacks

Are You Thinking What I'm Thinking?
A Patchwork Journey Through My Life... So Far

The final show of the season was a Saturday matinee at the Glen Street Theatre, nestled on Sydney's middle North Shore. Naughty Don Chapman and I cooked up a scheme... yes... real weed in Geoff's smoke for the very last performance. Marty, bless his clean-living heart, didn't touch the stuff. I managed to scrounge a little bit from a mate and carefully laced Geoff's reefer with it. Not too much, mind you; pepper and salt... just a touch. Don and I were lurking on the OP (opposite prompt) side of the stage, keeping an eye on the scene, which was going along beautifully despite the small, last-show matinee crowd. We could barely contain ourselves. Marty did know how to smoke cigarettes (must've done it in a show once) and used to elaborately draw the smoke into his lungs like a seasoned pro. And on this particular day, he reefed on that thing like there was no tomorrow. Don and I went silent, frozen in anticipation. Time seemed to slow down a bit after Marty had taken several massive drags... we saw the exact moment it hit him. Suddenly, his eyes widened, he was waving the joint around in the air, and the small but appreciative audience were absolutely roaring with laughter! Marty, ever the professional and to his absolute credit, manfully carried on to finish the scene without that wretched giggle-stick ever being raised to his slightly quivering lips again. Don and I raced down to the dressing rooms for the interval, laughing like a couple of lunatics. We waited for his arrival. I could hear him lurching down the hallway, he burst through the door, slammed it shut behind him, leaned back against it, absolutely howling with laughter.... Finally, he managed to get it out...

'YOU BASTARDS!!!!'

I mean, fair dinkum... you'd be chucked in the clink for something like that these days! Fortunately, Marty (the excellent professional and good sport that he is) threw cold water on his face, knocked back a coffee, straightened himself up, and went on to nail the rest of the performance like it had never been nailed before! We all went out for the wrap party and had a cracking night... so bloody funny. I hope he's been using that story for his entire career!

Are You Thinking What I'm Thinking? A Patchwork Journey Through My Life... So Far

Back to Stock Squad...

Kris McQuade

Gorgeous Kris McQuade was our leading lady. A NIDA graduate from way back in '71 and a strong, direct presence in absolutely everything she does. She was playing a straight-talking, slightly damaged country girl with a rough exterior but a heart of gold... a walk in the park for Krissy. This was the very first time I met her (we've worked together several times since). I wandered into the empty foyer of the production office in Sydney for a wardrobe fitting just as Krissy was leaving. I knew who she was and introduced myself, told her the name of the character I was playing, and stuck out my hand for a shake... she completely bypassed my right hand and then ever so gently cupped her right hand up high between my legs... as if to simply say a soft hello and... I dunno... surely not... feel if there was any weight there? It shocked the absolute hell out of me, but somehow I held my ground and didn't flinch.

Her eyes never left mine, and with that familiar slightly wicked smile of hers, she slowly drawled in that impossibly deep, sexy voice... 'Hello Kenny, I'm very pleased to meet you.' I did wonder for a moment if this was some kind of special theatrical greeting or just her standard way of saying hello... I really must ask her one day. We had a close, professional working relationship on several projects after that. I admire her work immensely. A terrific woman! Our first

Are You Thinking What I'm Thinking?
A Patchwork Journey Through My Life... So Far

encounter was ever so slightly confronting for yours truly, but somehow I managed to get through it...

The late, great Aussie stalwart Gerard Kennedy played the weary, slightly clumsy country copper, with Michael O'Neil as his young, keen offsider. Carmen Duncan was there too, along with Brendan Lunny and a few others. I played a cocky rural lad called Doug... all cowboy hat and attitude.

Howard Ruby was directing – (ready, set, action!) – and Ross Berryman was behind the camera – what a fantastic Director of Photography (DOP) and Camera Operator he is. I worked with him again not long after on an episode of *Butterfly Island*. That starred Grigor Taylor, who I'd admired ever since *Matlock Police* back in the 1970s. I thought he was a brilliant actor. A NIDA graduate from 1970, he had a strong, simple, and practical approach to the work. Very handsome, professional, and always consistent. We shot it at Mission Beach in Queensland. What an absolutely gorgeous location! Just one of the many trips I've had over the years to Queensland to film movies and mini-series. In *Butterfly Island*, I played a runaway robber called Mr Brown. Aviator sunnies and my shirt unbuttoned just a little bit too far, naturally.

The keen eye of Ross Berryman

Are You Thinking What I'm Thinking? A Patchwork Journey
Through My Life… So Far

The cinematographer is your friend (or should be…)

Ross also lensed the second series of *Fields of Fire* for Palm Beach Pictures and the Nine Network. He's had an absolutely amazing career and is such a quiet, gentle bloke. Exactly the type of cinematographer I love working with. Quietly practical, inventive, and patient. He brings a lovely sense of care and inclusiveness to the actor within his process, and a kind of professional respect that really resonates with me.

Not all DOPs and operators are like this. Plenty have a very much 'hands off the actor' approach. Barely give you a second glance and hardly ever utter a word. Some completely ignore you, which I find incredibly disconcerting. I mean, they're the ones looking right at you through the lens… they could offer so much support! A strong rapport with the DOP, and particularly the operator, can be an absolute lifesaver for your performance. They can be your best mate on set. I've worked with some clueless directors who've somehow managed to land the gig despite a complete lack of understanding about what might be needed within the actor's work. No language to use, no idea about the actor's process to draw upon, zero people skills, and a total inability to offer a useful direction that can be translated into action or physicality. In these situations, the operator and the actor can forge a silent connection, a coded way of working that can bypass a dud director… a little nod, a subtle, pursed-lip shake of the head… a raised, questioning eyebrow, a smile and a wink… performance-saving connections when the chips are down. Sometimes in this crazy game, we need to be director-proof.

My absolute favourite working environment is when everyone close to the camera is mindful, inclusive, and respectful. Tedious, rigid demarcation and hierarchical flexing of muscle really detract from the process. And on some sets, you can practically feel it in the air… so many egos crammed into a tight space. When the vibe close to the camera is like that, it's such a waste of energy and really hinders the creative flow. Thankfully, I've worked on many projects where the collaboration is genuine and thorough, respectful and supportive. When it is, the creative juices flow freely from all departments, and little bits of storytelling magic can happen day after day. What a pleasure it is to work in that kind of environment. On a bigger project, you can have hundreds of people... literally hundreds of people working together towards the common goal of telling a story well. It's a wonderful feeling to be part of that. At its best, there's often a feeling of quiet joy and contentment floating over the set. Folks pitch in and help each other out, have a laugh, crack jokes, keep things light, and rib each other good-naturedly. And in that lighter atmosphere, there seems to be so much more room for a kind of free expression in creativity. I've had so many moments of quiet joy in the true collaboration that filmmaking can be.

Leadership

Overwhelmingly, that respectful, inclusive atmosphere comes straight from the top. It's the essence of the humanist 'trickle-down' effect. If the Producers lead from the front and embody this mindset and this style of human interaction, then inevitably and quite naturally that quiet respect filters down through the heads of department. The knock-on effect ripples throughout the entire production because the people at the top, the ones holding the purse strings, operate with expert leadership qualities.

I've worked in many different industries and studied and worked within various educational institutions. My observations and experience of high-quality leadership have been presented to me time and time again, and almost always in exactly the same way. The same principles apply whether you're working in a team of carpenters, as a telemarketer in a hugely successful online wine-selling company, running around with a team of A-grade AFL umpires, or acting in a multi-million-dollar feature film. Clear communication, active listening, care, and respect. Treat people like adults, give them responsibility, let them get on with their job, and be kind. Surround yourself with people who are better than you at their job, have people raise the bar for you as a leader... and always think before you speak.

A Little More on Leadership... Janet

I was tour and stage manager for a couple of productions commissioned and developed by the now-disbanded, Mt Gambier-based regional company, Mainstreet Theatre, in the early to mid-2000s. One of these was an excellent one-man show called *The Lightkeeper*. The Artistic Director, Teresa Bell, commissioned Verity Laughton to write the piece and cast the wonderful Ian Scott as the lightkeeper. Scotty is a NIDA grad from '75. A beautiful soul (sickeningly handsome, as his hilarious wife Elizabeth once quipped), a great actor, and an ordinary but improving carpenter. Another wonderful friendship and working relationship for lucky old me.

We were scheduled to set up and perform the piece at the fabulous Vasse Felix winery in Margaret River, Western Australia, in March 2005. The winery was, and probably still is, owned by Janet Holmes à Court. At the time, I recall she was listed as the wealthiest woman in Australia. She was a true champion of the arts and had a reputation as a most generous and approachable person. The winery had stunningly beautiful grounds. The gardeners we passed gave us a big welcoming wave as we rumbled by in the ute, lugging the overladen trailer containing everything for the show. We said a quick hello to the happy, helpful folks at reception, then I unhooked the trailer and dropped Scotty at the accommodation in the town proper so he could rest and prepare – it was a big gig for him, and he needed to gather his strength during the day for the vigorous journey of the piece every night. I was so proud of his work in this play. One man and a big story on a simple set that represented the top of the lighthouse... brilliantly directed by Teresa, with an excellent set design by Steve Jankowicz and sound design by the fabulous David Franzke. It was an excellent piece of theatre. Teresa, who was the innovative Artistic Director of the company, had a great idea to tour the play through coastal areas, sometimes playing in marquees set up under actual lighthouses

Are You Thinking What I'm Thinking?
A Patchwork Journey Through My Life… So Far

throughout Western Australia, South Australia, and Victoria. Scotty and I travelled from gig to gig in the underpowered ute, towing a huge, heavy tandem trailer chock-full of lights, set, sound gear, props, and costumery. I would set it all up and pull it all down in my role as tour and stage manager. What a wonderful time it was to spend with dear Scotty and admire his commitment and detailed approach to the work. I'd offer him little thoughts and notes from time to time and make sure there was an ice-cold beer waiting for him after the show. I enjoyed and rose to the responsibility of looking after him as best I could. Only a small gig… playing to between twenty and two hundred or so people depending on the night and the location. Sometimes in a wind-blown marquee right on the coast, sometimes in the tiny mechanics institute hall of a small town, finishing up in the iconic Griffin Theatre. Excellent Aussie theatre. A real credit to Verity Laughton and Teresa Bell, and of course to dear Scotty.

The excellent Ian Scott, brilliant as The Lightkeeper for Mainstreet Theatre.

Are You Thinking What I'm Thinking? A Patchwork Journey Through My Life... So Far

It was an early show at the winery. Gorgeous late afternoon sun, stunning architecture, a captivated audience, and good old Scotty absolutely on his game. Rapturous applause and slaps on the back all round! Janet then invited Scotty and me to join her and her partner at a cool, casual eatery in Margaret River. A lovely time was had by all, with great food, wine, and stories being shared. Janet was charming and generous, of course, genuinely interested in Ian and me and our tales of film, theatre, NIDA, and the 'unusual' life of being an actor in Australia. I was particularly curious about the strong sense of well-being and camaraderie I felt so keenly from her staff at the winery. From the gardener's welcoming wave as we drove past in the ute to the pleasant, helpful, and creative assistance offered by every single member of her 'team' at Vasse Felix. I pointed out what a happy workplace it seemed to be. I'd read somewhere that the value of the holdings she was responsible for had doubled since the passing of her husband. She shared a story with me that I've never forgotten, one that really echoed my own thoughts on leadership. She said, 'Well, it is a beautiful location... but there's something more to it. Something I'm quite proud of, actually. My husband passed away some years ago and left me solely in charge of quite a substantial group of companies. I'm becoming more of a businessperson now, but that wasn't always the case. What I was, and what I still am, is a people person. I'm a great reader of people. I'm genuinely interested in people. This is how I operate, and it's what I believe is the key to any success I'm responsible for, both in business and in life: I employ really good people. I look after them very well. I let them get on with their job, and I always ask them what they think.... Thank you and Ian for a most wonderful theatrical experience.'

It was quite a profound little moment for me. What a simple, honest, and humanistic philosophy. Again, the collaboration on a storytelling journey yielded such great rewards, in the most unexpected ways. When I discuss the importance of storytelling with students, this type of experience is exactly what I mean. Art sneaks up on you;

Are You Thinking What I'm Thinking?
A Patchwork Journey Through My Life... So Far

philosophy, the human condition, the shared experiences, and the discoveries available to all of us are everywhere in these places.

I got to tour manage and stage manage this show, watch and work with Scotty as he navigated the journey of the piece nightly, meet all sorts of interesting folks along the way, and soak in the glow and the feeling created for the audiences. When I say to students and teachers that storytellers make better carpenters, better bus drivers, better doctors, better police officers, better teachers, better Prime Ministers... this is what I mean. The stories and the collaborations enhance our life experience and our understanding of each other.

I really am sneaking up on a couple of Priscilla stories...

The next time I saw Stephan after *Stock Squad* was around 1993 at a party in Paddington. He was enthusiastically describing a film he was incredibly excited about writing and directing – following three drag queens on a bus trip through the outback. He said, probably not entirely truthfully, that he hadn't cast the leads yet. So, naturally, I told him I was absolutely perfect for one of the drag queens and gave him a quick, impromptu, sort of audition in the form of a story... oh dear, how very uncool of me!

William Street on a quiet night

Are You Thinking What I'm Thinking? A Patchwork Journey Through My Life... So Far

On a wet Tuesday night in May 1993, I was striding up William Street near Kings Cross after a top-notch feed at Bill and Tony's following umpire training. Headed up and over the hill to weave my way down to my digs. I was living in a tiny cottage in Roylston Street, Paddington, right across the road from Trumper Park – a cute little cricket and football oval, and the home ground of the East Sydney Bulldogs Aussie rules club. I'll tell you more about Trumper another time. I was pretty fit back then, running around with the senior squad of the New South Wales Australian Football League Umpires. I was a reasonably quick runner in those years too – clocked an 'explosive' hand-held 12.3 seconds over one hundred metres at the Kensington running track one training night... So, head held high, kit bag over the shoulder, I spotted a working 'girl' up ahead. William Street was chock-a-block with street-working transsexuals in those days, sometimes with lines of cars stretching the entire length of the street heading down towards Crown Street. Windows down, girls leaning into the passenger side, negotiating prices, and the blokes behind the wheel checking out the 'talent.' When I was driving cabs around that time, I remember having four or five country blokes in the car, well and truly on the turps. They asked me to cruise down William Street past the 'ladies of the night'... There was some very revealing costumery on display down that street back then. I waited until the boys had stopped their oohing and aahing before quietly enlightening them,

'They're blokes.'

'What?'

'They're blokes... all of 'em – well, sort of half and half really...'

They ordered me to do another lap, go around again... they loved it. I mean, these 'girls' were very attractive, and at that moment, Combined Cab 73 was full of alcohol-fuelled possibility. Sydney was laying it all out for these rural chaps, and the forbidden fruit was a definite temptation...

'Slow down, mate, slow down... Jesus... are they really blokes?'

Are You Thinking What I'm Thinking?
A Patchwork Journey Through My Life… So Far

'Yeah, beautiful blokes with breasts… you want me to drop you here, gentlemen, or take you up to the Gazebo?'

'Nah, take us down to Harry's, mate, we'll get a pie.'

Stick with me, dear reader… I'm telling Stephan the story of my approach towards the lone transsexual. It was a quiet winter Tuesday, so business would have been a bit slow, for sure. As I got closer, I could see she was going to have a crack at me (so to speak). Nothing new in that; if you lived near the Cross in those days, it was a regular occurrence. This particular gal, however, was reasonably unusual in that there was very little resemblance to actually being a woman. Little burgundy-coloured mini-dress, fluffy short black jacket, badly dyed red hair piled up in a messy, floppy bun, frighteningly thick eye makeup, red lips, very tall and shiny high heels. Through the fishnet stockings, there was thick black leg hair, and it was confirmed: those sturdy legs were strangers to the razor. The high heels would have been a bloke's size eleven, her hands were huge, her face had a three-day growth, and she had the slightly surly, resentful look of a working girl very much in need of a customer. I was the only walker, and she was the only worker. She approached me square on, and with a rather confrontational, wild-eyed look, she enquired in a steady, measured, raspy, deep male timbre,

'You want a girl?'

I couldn't help it… it just happened… it was involuntary… I laughed. Well, it was more like a high-pitched yelp, really. Much louder than it should have been and very disrespectful. She was bigger than me and pretty wound up… so my old, natural, evasive football skills instinctively kicked in. I executed what used to be known as the baulk, followed by the blind turn, spun around her like a young Bobby Skilton (nimble South Melbourne player), and bolted up the street. She would never have caught me in those heels – I was a senior umpire, after all! I was off like a dog with its tail between its legs, bursting through centre half-forward with the big sticks looming. Bang! Straight up the

Are You Thinking What I'm Thinking? A Patchwork Journey Through My Life... So Far

hill towards the Kings Cross fire station, quietly giggling my stupid head off.

I thought I told this story pretty well to Stephan... with my impersonation of the working girl surely bound to nail me the role of one of the trannies on the bus. He stared blankly at me for a while, then just carried on partying... So much for that!

A while later, the agent rang to tell me there was an offer on the table for a role in *Priscilla*. Frank, an incredibly hot (yeah, right), slightly naïve country chap who happens across one of the drag queens at a drive-in party in Coober Pedy. I read the sequence and thought, 'Oh alright, I'll do it.' Frank is probably the darkest character in the picture, falling for Felicia Jollygoodfellow (played by the fabulous Guy Pearce) at the drive-in. She's 'working the room' a bit and wondering out loud who might be available to show her around the town. Frank, quietly enamoured by this exotic creature, shyly offers,

'It'd be a pleasure.'

Frank and Felicia Jollygoodfellow. He can't believe his luck

He's clearly smitten by her and a bit taken aback by the whole encounter, until he clocks the size of her hands and those rather impressive biceps Guy Pearce was sporting back then. Oooo... looks like trouble's brewing... She throws a drink right in his face and legs it. Frank and his goons chase after her, eventually cornering her next to a shed. Frank then delivers a hefty right hook to her jaw, orders his cronies to open her legs, and yells at Bob (played by Billy Hunter) to get out of the way... he's just about to plant a boot right where it really hurts when he's interrupted by Terence Stamp's character, Bernadette...

Terence Stamp Misses The Target... Or Does He?

We shot this sequence in and around the old drive-in cinema just outside Coober Pedy, in central South Australia. It's a place famous for its fringe dwellers, misfits, and opal miners. I arrived on a Thursday afternoon, chatting pleasantly to the driver as we closed in on the main street. The shoot itself had been challenging, constantly on the move, and the budget was barely enough to make it all happen smoothly. Everyone was working for minimum money. Heads of department were on 'back-end' points in the picture, a kind of deferred wage, as were the main actors. They all did fabulously from that back-end deal further down the track, when the picture became a global hit, which is great! Me? "$600 for your contribution is all we can afford, Radley... sorry..." Of course, they could actually have afforded more, but they simply weren't going to pay it. My hard-nosed agent probably earned her 10% by dragging them up from $550.

A hot, low sun cast bright light down the main drag, giving it an old-fashioned, cowboy western feel. It was dusty, slightly unsettling. As we eased down the street, an ominous atmosphere settled. There were a lot of young, indigenous fellas around, quite wild, wound up and agitated. They were drinking beers and yelling. Suddenly, one bloke chased another onto the road right in front of us. They were screaming at each other. The chaser grabbed the other bloke, threw him violently onto the road, then punched him repeatedly with hammer blows. It was awful.

Other guys came over and pulled the thumping bloke off, dragging him away. I was horrified. The driver remarked, "It's Thursday; they've just been paid. It's welfare day. Some of them go and blow it all on booze

Are You Thinking What I'm Thinking? A Patchwork Journey Through My Life... So Far

immediately and punch the shit out of each other." He slowly continued down the street. I was genuinely shaken.

Then, up ahead at the next intersection, a man crossed the street. The warm, late afternoon sun shone on him. He had silver hair and tanned skin, wearing loose, cream linen trousers and a jacket with a T-shirt underneath, and classy sandals. It was like a vision from Morocco or the Greek Isles. This lone figure of style and sophistication, gliding across the road looking for all the world like a Vogue model or... a movie star.

"Who's that?" I asked.

"That's Terence Stamp."

So, Bernadette (played by Terence) thankfully interrupts the impending awful moment of Frank sinking the boot into Felicia.

"Stop flexing your muscles, you big pile of budgie turd. I'm sure your mates will be much more impressed if you just go back to the pub and fuck a couple of pigs on the bar."

Bob (Bill Hunter's character) calls her name. Frank clocks this, then continues with, "Bernadette! The whole circus is in town! I s'pose you want a fuck too? Come on, Bernadette. Come and fuck me... that's it... come on... come and fuck me... fuck me."

She walks right up to him, smiles her delightful, cheeky smile, then lifts her knee powerfully up between his legs. Twice. Frank drops in a heap. She flicks her hair back and announces... "There. Now you're fucked."

The scene is the darkest and most dangerous moment in the picture. Homophobia is presented so clearly out there in Coober Pedy. This scene has become quite an iconic moment in Aussie film. It was used in George Miller's documentary on Australian cinema, and likewise, in David Stratton's Australian cinema. I've seen it elsewhere too. The homophobe gets what's coming to him. An iconic scene in an iconic picture.

Are You Thinking What I'm Thinking?
A Patchwork Journey Through My Life... So Far

When we were setting up the climax of the scene, there were stuntmen on set to guide Terence and myself through the knee moment. Over my career, I've always found stunties to be a great support; they can help you stay safe and make you look like you know what you're doing. For this moment, they advised I wear undies pulled up very tight! I actually can't remember if a cricket 'box' was involved. They did feed a strong piece of army-style webbing up the inside of my trouser leg, over the gusset, and down the other inside leg. The webbing was pulled down firmly on each side, and a strong piece of Velcro was wrapped around the ankle of each leg to ensure plenty of downward pressure on the crotch of the trousers, thereby creating a kind of fabric rebound platform. The idea was that if Terence's aim was slightly off, his knee would strike the stretched trouser gusset rather than my 'wedding tackle' (as those ABC legends Roy and H.G. used to describe the area). A great idea, in my opinion. The stunties also trained Terence on how to strike the inside of my upper thigh with a slightly diagonal knee lift direction. There was plenty of rehearsal for Terence with the stunties, and the lads had a word with me on how one might collapse when struck in this manner. As I said, they can make you look authentic at moments like that.

Thankfully, we only did one take of this moment. Terence went right up the middle... twice. Oof. Oof! The collapse you see and the groan you hear are 100% authentic. No acting required. It was an 'act-free' zone. It took me a little while to compose myself and stand. The nurse couldn't do much for me, of course, apart from offering a little sympathy. Terence was most apologetic.

"That's alright," I squeaked in a weird, high-pitched voice as I gently worked my nuts down to their correct resting place from somewhere up around my belly button. A little while later, Terence came to check on me, apologised again, and invited me to lunch later that day. I was glad he made that offer, as he'd actually been quite reckless in that moment. Care, always care for your fellow actors. I accepted the invite...

Are You Thinking What I'm Thinking? A Patchwork Journey Through My Life... So Far

Terence Stamp

Later that day, we met in one of those amazing underground caves for an excellent meal. The place was run by a very urban, attractive German couple who were, of course, fussing over Terence and offering brilliant service. The food was first-class. How are such fresh ingredients available so far from a major city? The answer: aircraft and refrigeration. We chatted about the business and our various partners and offspring. It was a really pleasant occasion. I then joined Terence for what he said would be his final visit to a wholesale opal dealer. Coober Pedy is a major mining and dealing town for opals. He explained that he was starting to annoy the seller as he didn't want to pay the asking price and was in the midst of a hardball negotiation. The seller probably thought, 'movie star = very wealthy.' That may well have been true, although I knew Terence wasn't getting paid much for his initial work on the picture. One of the producers, a rather wild chap called Michael Hamlyn (a son of the huge greeting card company), probably quite inappropriately said to me at the time, "You'd be shocked if you knew what Terence was being paid for this." "I doubt it, love... I'm shocked at what I'm being paid!" I thought, but didn't say. The opal was enormous – an amazing, beautiful blue, shimmering thing. I felt slightly uncomfortable being there, but

Are You Thinking What I'm Thinking?
A Patchwork Journey Through My Life... So Far

Terence didn't care at all. I actually forget the figures they were throwing about, but we left without the sale going through. As we wandered down the street to the hotel, Terence chuffed, "I'll ring him later and tell him I'll pay it." Hollywood hardball dealt out by T. Stamp... A very nice chap. I think he was voted most handsome man in the Universe at one stage too. He certainly dressed nicely.

So, *Priscilla* opens and creates a storm of interest around the world. It also picks up many awards: an Oscar for Best Costume Design, won by Lizzie Gardiner and Tim Chappel; a Best Costume Design BAFTA for Lizzie and Tim; a Best Makeup BAFTA for Cassie Hanlon and Angela Conte Strykermeyer. Many other nominations and wins occurred all over the world. According to IMDb, the picture grossed at least 20 times its budget in box office receipts. It's had an amazing life. Many people have told me it's their favourite Australian film. It was a terrific piece of luck to be involved in this picture. When folks ask me, 'What have you been in?' these days I start with *Pirates*, *The Power of The Dog*, *The New Boy*, *Force of Nature*... but then!... good old *Priscilla*. Most people have seen it, and most people love it. I, of course, never mention what I was paid. So many people think that just because you're in film, TV, or indeed Bananas, you're automatically wealthy and very financially comfortable... Not true at all. Who'd be an actor for the money?

My last little moment to share is a tiny one. At the hugely flamboyant opening night party held at FOX Studios Sydney, I felt slightly overwhelmed by the bigness of it all and didn't stay very long. I'm not fond of crowds. I just stayed for the amazing opening number and the speeches. There were hundreds of drag queens and trannies about, just having an absolute ball. It was an amazing, 'big' occasion.

I was approached by a particularly butch, familiar-looking drag lady... red hair up, incredible eye makeup, solid legs, fishnets, and huge hands. She said in a gruff, deep voice, "So, did working on this film broaden your mind, sweetheart?" I replied, "Oh, it was already reasonably broad... but now maybe it's a little broader... I think."

Are You Thinking What I'm Thinking? A Patchwork Journey Through My Life… So Far

"Have a good night, handsome." "Thanks, you too." I had a quick hello chat to Hugo then left.

Holden 1977 H.G Wagon, and farewell to Doughboy – an absolute shitheap. Full of rust, wandered all over the road, leaked both water and dust. I used it for tools and eventually for a Sydney/Melbourne road trip with my girlfriend. Part of this journey was for Mum and Dad to meet Rita in Kyneton, which all went really well, of course. Then a journey to Cohuna. My uncle Ken, after whom I was named, was dealing with stage 4 cancer and didn't have long to go. He was a jolly rascal of a man, a baker all his life with the nickname 'Doughboy' – folks say it was the flour and dust in the air of the bakery for so many years that had brought on the cancer. Mum and Dad had warned me – 'he's not like the Doughy you knew'… and of course, he wasn't. So skinny and slow and hunched. But somehow, the laugh, the jolly, the smile, the charm was bursting. It was an amazing visit. We had a sandwich, a cup of tea and a quiet catchup. He somehow hobbled outside to wave us off, all of us knowing it was the last time. He stood as tall as he could manage out on the nature strip, arm extended fully with the biggest grin, 'See you again!' he hollered as we eased off down the road. It was such a powerful moment. I pulled the beige beast over when we rounded the corner. I couldn't drive any further for a while. We were both in tears at this very personal and wonderful and sad moment. My namesake, the very man I was named after, had said his final goodbye to us… but it wasn't goodbye. It was a call to the future… Oh dear. The dignified bravery. Goodbye Doughy, you are a gem.

We then spent New Year's Eve 1989 on a lonesome dirt road in the Victorian high country, somewhere around the Corryong grazing area, under brilliant stars with the car covered in streamers and a bottle of cheap booze… classic Aussie road trip. I finally took the plates off this car, left it parked over the road in Roylston Street, Paddo – clearly alone and abandoned. To my happy astonishment, over a period of time, the car was completely stripped of wheels, panels, steering wheel, and engine parts. It felt so good to know that the old dear had spread its love around to various places! The council eventually took the shell away to be crushed and used as something else. A feeling of virtuosity pervaded over this matter! Recycling an old beast!

Holden Wagon 1976

WAR! What did you do it for?

A change of heart and the circle of life...

My Dad, Donald Radley (no middle name), was born in 1927. He was one of nine children. He was twelve when WW2 broke out in 1939. I think he actually joined up in 1945, just as the war was ending. I know he did his training at an Army base camp at Canungra, near Witheren in Queensland. From the little he told us, it was known as a very tough place to undergo the thirteen weeks of basic training allotted to new recruits at that time. To have 'gone through Canungra' meant you had endured one of the toughest basic training regimes given to new recruits in the Australian Army at that point. With all recruits, no matter what your specific role in the A.D.F., the principle remains: you are a soldier first, a mechanic second, a driver second, an accountant second, and so on. If you are a soldier, you are a soldier as required.

Are You Thinking What I'm Thinking? A Patchwork Journey Through My Life... So Far

Private Donald Radley, ready to serve his country

Dad was a cook in the Army. He served in Rabaul during what was known as 'the cleanup'. The clean-up of Rabaul, among other tasks, involved searching for and capturing Japanese soldiers hiding on the island, some of whom may not have known of the surrender. My Dad was involved in this. In what way, I do not actually know.

It's too bloody late, I know, but I wish I'd had so many conversations with Dad about his life. I can't now; the moment, or moments, have passed.

He, like so many soldiers of his generation, spoke little of the war to his family. He was fiercely proud and protective of the work he and his comrades did over those awful years. But he never spoke of what he did there. Two members of the Kyneton RSL were present at his funeral in 2010. I was so proud of him through the immensely respectful words they spoke. They uttered the simple words, 'he saw action'. That's all we need to know. He represented his country. He put his life on the line such that we might retain our freedom and protect

Are You Thinking What I'm Thinking?
A Patchwork Journey Through My Life... So Far

our place. They, all of them, did what was right, and I am so proud and humbled by what he did, and all of our servicemen and women in all of the wars, and in all of their capacities.

Dad was President of the Kyneton RSL for a time. He held the position with distinction and dignity. He marched every year in the ANZAC parade. In the end, it was not so much marching as shuffling, getting along somehow, with a walker. Always with head held high and the look of solid determination that earned him the affectionate nickname 'Bulldog'.

The American war in Vietnam was an incredibly divisive time within Australia. We, as a country, had been so grateful for America's support during the Second World War that we immediately followed them into Korea, then Vietnam. They saved us from the Japanese invasion – we would support them in the halting of the 'red menace' – the steady flood of Chinese communism oozing its way south with the domino effect through North Vietnam. Any Baby Boomers or older folk reading this will be aware of **Conscription**. For those that don't know – there was a Federal Government policy operating in Australia. Between 1965 and 1972, almost all Australian men at 19/20 years of age were, by law, required to register for **National Service**. They were known as 'Nashos'.

It was a lottery. The Government selected numbers from a rotating drum. If the number correlated to your birthday, you were informed by official Commonwealth Government letter and, by law, you were required to register for National Service. That is, join the Army. Your number came up – that's it, you're in the Army... for three years.

The arguments at the dinner table about this whole thing were passionate. My sister Jane was completely anti-war, as I recall. My Dad was 100% supportive of the 'Nasho' scheme and our involvement in the war, because he knew what the horror of war meant and believed the threat of the approaching commies... The war was on TV every night, the first televised war: American choppers, huge explosions, napalm, horror upon horror...

Are You Thinking What I'm Thinking? A Patchwork Journey Through My Life... So Far

Anti War protest in Melbourne

I didn't know what to think. My mind was on becoming a football champion, on motorbikes, girls, and music; I simply wanted to be liked by everyone! I had three square meals every day, incredible music on the radio. At Eltham High School, a new, exciting curriculum was taking shape, alongside social change, flower power, and the anticipation of Woodstock... Phew, what an era!

Dad had steadfastly aligned himself with what he saw as the principle of this horrific war. For him, supporting America was our unequivocal duty. The fear of Communist expansion was profoundly real to my father, and he wasn't alone. The 'red menace' was genuinely perceived as a threat to America. A quick glance at the Jacaranda atlas clearly showed where the 'commies' were headed: southeast, towards the wide brown land, laden with resources and space for those 'awful' Asian people to inhabit.

Australia was still in the grip of the 'White Australia' policy. The Immigration Restriction Act, one of the first Commonwealth laws passed after Federation in 1901, aimed to limit non-white (particularly Asian) immigration to Australia, thereby helping to keep Australia 'British'. The fearful, protectionist racism and xenophobia upon which this policy was built, and which it further entrenched, was never stronger than between the end of the Second World War and the early

Are You Thinking What I'm Thinking?
A Patchwork Journey Through My Life... So Far

1970s. My dear father was brought up amidst the very strongest currents of xenophobia and racism.

From his childhood in Cohuna Victoria, right up to the 1970s and beyond Aboriginal Australians were disregarded, disrespected, and treated appallingly. Having fought against the terrible onslaught of the Japanese in the Second World War, he was steadfast in his strong dislike of Asians generally, and understandably held a deep loathing for the Japanese specifically, alongside a disregard for Indigenous Australians.

The arguments around the dinner table regarding National Service and our involvement in America's war with Vietnam, particularly those from my sister, were passionate and heated. I remember saying I didn't want to join the discussion because I 'didn't know enough about it'. I didn't march in the anti-war moratorium in May 1970; the thought of it frightened me. I was not yet thirteen, so I suppose that makes sense. More than 200,000 people across Australia marched and held rallies to demonstrate their wish for us to immediately pull our troops out of Vietnam. Dad, through all of this, was quietly conflicted. As a matter of principle and through his own experience, he sided with America and their 'strong-arm international diplomacy'. Yet, at the same time, he was a strong advocate for the power of people banding together through the union movement to achieve better wages and conditions for workers. He was a Labour man, a worker, a team man. The wedge of this unwinnable war, driven into our society, undoubtedly caused him great internal conflict.

Many years later, when my ageing parents were living in a lovely old home in Kyneton, Victoria, I was there for one of their fabulous Sunday roasts. The table was set traditionally, with roses in the vase, amazing pork and crackling, perfect gravy, and beautifully cooked vegetables. These were absolutely delicious meals; we all loved them. My mouth still waters at the memory.

The conversation briefly traversed America's current international war efforts. President Ronald Reagan had decided to intervene in the Iran-

Are You Thinking What I'm Thinking? A Patchwork Journey Through My Life... So Far

Iraq War, with undeclared US involvement, using massive naval and air power in support of Saddam Hussein. The American war machine was showing its might yet again. We chatted briefly about the USA's consistent tendency to flex its military muscle wherever it saw fit – both overtly and covertly. The war in Vietnam was then brought up. My dear Dad, after all those years and all that strong opinion held throughout the sixties and seventies, quietly announced to all of us at the table: 'I was wrong. We shouldn't have been involved in that war. Our men died over there under our flag in a war that did not involve us... I was wrong.' Again, I beamed with pride for my father. The man who had served his country against a real threat coming south from Asia wanted to share with us that he had been mistaken. It meant so much to me.

The Last Goodbye

I missed my dad's death by minutes. I'd been summoned from wherever I was – I can't remember where now – and broke speed limits to reach Kyneton Hospital, where he was on his last legs. The nurse at reception wouldn't let me pass at first; she seemed confused as to who I was. 'Just have a look at me, Sister,' I urged, 'who do I look like?' I raced into the room, but he had just gone. Then another nurse asked my sister Jane if she might give Dad a shave to tidy him up a little, so I waited. My son, Angus, and daughter, Georgia, arrived with their mother, Rita. My two younger children Marvin and Angelica were with their mother in NSW at the time. There's that strange hiatus after the departed actually leave... they're gone. They were, and now they are not. We can't do anything about it; we can't change it. A quiet calm and stillness settled over us just then. The nurse came out and nodded, indicating Dad was ready for a final goodbye. She was magnificent – have I said this? Nurses are angels (mostly). It was time to see my dear father for the last time. My then fourteen-year-old boy, Angus, was standing with me. I asked him if he'd like to come in. He nodded. We saw this giant in our lives lying still and peacefully. Angus said quietly, 'What a beast.' I think what he meant was, what a sight, what a presence, what a moment. It was so brave of him to experience that

Are You Thinking What I'm Thinking?
A Patchwork Journey Through My Life... So Far

with me. Profound, for him, for me, for us both. Dad was resting. Pa is resting. The big sleep.

My father's funeral service was held on a sunny day, November 7th 2010, in Kyneton, Victoria. I read a short eulogy, some of which I shall include in these writings. Dad was buried next to my mother, who had died about eighteen months before. She had passed away from old age, worn out and suffering from alcohol-induced dementia. Dad, though still sharp-witted, had a body that had simply given out after a lifetime of hard work and so much sport. Diabetes had compromised him for ten or fifteen years prior to his death. It was a lovely send-off at Kyneton cemetery. We placed some personal, meaningful things on his coffin, lowered him in, threw rose petals, shed tears, held each other, and quietly stood for a time to reflect personally and simply feel for this man and the profound part he played in all our lives. It was a sad, yet beautiful, moment. Slowly, the congregation began to leave. I was the second-to-last person to walk away that day. The very last person stood silently at the head of my father's grave, head bowed, back ramrod straight. This was Mr Guy Williamson, my nephew, the youngest son of my sister Jane and her quirky, clever husband, Graeme. Guy had been very close to Dad throughout his entire life. He'd left high school in year ten or eleven, having absolutely struggled to fit into the archaic Victorian education system. He applied for, and was accepted into, the Royal Australian Air Force – the only person in Dad's life or family who had joined the ADF. Guy completed his high school education, studied to become an aircraft mechanic, and remained in the RAAF for many years. He still works as an aircraft mechanic and is brilliant at his job. So, there he was, in full dress uniform, on a sunny day in Kyneton, to send off his wonderful Pa. I had turned as I wandered off; I saw this vision of a man click his heels to attention, his uniform immaculate. Then he somehow rose even taller, snapping out the most perfect salute I have ever seen. It was in honour of this great man, and I could feel how incredibly proud he would have been of his grandson in that amazing moment. Guy held the salute for the longest time, like a well-lit statue in the most

Are You Thinking What I'm Thinking? A Patchwork Journey Through My Life... So Far

powerful cinematic crossover of life and death. He then perfectly dropped that right arm – 'the shortest way home', Dad used to say – turned sharply on his heels, and walked, or perhaps marched, away, leaving that huge moment hanging in the air. It was the most powerful, moving thing I have ever witnessed and will stay with me forever.

Dad's last ANZAC day march, with his Grandson

Leading Aircraft Man Guy Williamson,

Royal Australian Air Force

The Legacy Of My Father

Below is part of the eulogy I wrote and read at my father's funeral on November 7th, 2010.

What a generous big heart was beating in that chest. His good will and love for family and extended family was enormous. Everybody felt at ease with him - man, woman and child. A big welcome, a lovely meal with lots of laughs, a hamper of goodies to take home and he and Mum would always stay out on the street and wave until we were out of sight.

Are You Thinking What I'm Thinking?
A Patchwork Journey Through My Life... So Far

He was proud of each and every member of his family, yes for what they achieved but mainly for who they are. He glowed with pride for all of us in the small goals of our lives - He only ever gave me one piece of advice: The dog always bites; the horse always kicks and the gun is always loaded.... I reminded him of it recently but he couldn't remember giving it.... It had meant a lot to me and still does.

I keep hearing his voice. 'Hi Ken'. I won't ever forget the sound.

He was brave and sensible in the last months of his life, getting his affairs in order and doing what he could to feel comfortable enough to leave this world and be with Mum. 'I've never looked at another woman', he said to me once and there is absolutely no doubt it was true. He missed her terribly in the 18 months since she passed away.

I can't remember ever building a billy cart, going on camping trips or working on the internal combustion engine with him. (he actually used to swear at inanimate objects like they had it in for him) He worked 3 jobs for 15 years for goodness' sake! What time or energy would there have been to do those things? He passed on no secrets of mechanical prowess, tricks of construction, bushman skills, hunting techniques or the like.

The gifts he gave me he didn't even know he was giving. I certainly didn't at the time. He led by example and taught me through his actions and unwavering commitment and natural attention to providing - yes, providing food, shelter and protection - but providing the space and permission to be who I was and to do what called me. And if it didn't work out? He was there to listen and be compassionate and supportive - without fail.

I feel I have a strong love for my children, my family and the ones close to me - And that strong love was taught to me, it was the great gift my father gave to me.

I will miss him so and I burst with pride and good fortune to be his son.

Are You Thinking What I'm Thinking? A Patchwork Journey Through My Life... So Far

Yamaha XT 250cc (1985) road/trail bike.

I still own this old thing, a Yamaha XT 250cc road/trail bike, tucked away in my daughter Georgia's shed. I picked it up for $500 from Damien K, a gentleman who lived further up the hill from my rough little shack in Campbells Creek. My hope in buying it was to encourage my kids to come and stay, to putt around the hundred acres my small rental sat on. It almost worked. They came a couple of times and had a bit of fun on the tired old four-stroke. I even have some happy footage to prove it.

But kids grow up, don't they? They move on, just like I did, and begin to live their own lives. To be honest, I'm pretty lonely a lot of the time, especially after spending twenty-four years or so doing it all: nappies, patting them to sleep, bathing, cooking meals, driving them around when they were little. Almost all my non-working time was dedicated to kid matters in some way or another. I did my best as an absent father, managing access weekends, school holidays, and so on.

Then what? They grow up. They move on. I still haven't really learnt to accept or sufficiently balance my own little world since everything changed a couple of short years ago. Time ticks by; we adjust as best we can and do our utmost to remember: the secret of life is enjoying the passage of time.

Are You Thinking What I'm Thinking?
A Patchwork Journey Through My Life... So Far

1985 Yamaha XT 250

A rough headed social game of footy. Panton Hill, Victoria circa late 1970's. I'm in there somewhere.

Are You Thinking What I'm Thinking? A Patchwork Journey Through My Life… So Far

Footy

'The older I get, the better I was'… I don't know who coined that phrase, but I'll happily claim it and run with it. We were undeniably a footy family. Carlton was *our* team, a bedrock of loyalty. Until, that is, my brother John—affectionately known as Fred for many years—committed the unthinkable: he defected to the unimaginable. Collingwood. Perhaps that stark black and white mirrors his view of the world? Who cares? He remains a traitor, and whether he likes it or not, the stirring words to the Blues' team song will forever be embedded in his unfortunate brain.

At around six feet one, John became a formidable ruck-rover, hard-man full-back type of player for Eltham—the Panthers, sporting Essendon colours—in his formative years. Later, he relocated to Adelaide, where he played for some Crow-eating mob for many seasons, enjoying considerable success and countless Saturday night 'gatherings'. These were dedicated to dissecting the game, toasting victories, or, inevitably, licking wounds. His team might have snared a premiership, and he even managed to win an award or two. I can't quite recall what for, but I'm fairly certain he only *just* deserved them. He also excelled at Baseball for Glenelg in South Australia, carving out a stellar career as both catcher and resident shit-stirrer. He's a biggish bloke with a booming voice, a firm stare, and a hard, straight right. He could certainly fight—though 'only if he had to'—and he absolutely loves a good story and a BBQ. These days, he hobbles around reasonably well on buggered knees. Years of chasing the pigskin and squatting endlessly with a catcher's mitt will, inevitably, compromise one's knees. He still barracks for Collingwood, the poor bugger. He *wants* to return to the Blues, but the really sad thing is, he doesn't even realise he wants to. Consequently, he exists in a confused fog that he'll probably never fathom. Poor bastard. I feel sorry for him, but only a tiny bit. Collingwood supporters, when all the whinging and bagging of umpires has died down, finally get what they deserve… oh, and yes, I did convert to the mighty Sydney Swans many years later… but that of course, is an entirely different matter. It must be said,

Are You Thinking What I'm Thinking?
A Patchwork Journey Through My Life... So Far

however, that brother John has always been good to me, and thank Christ he can take a joke!

My brother Pete, meanwhile, briefly swapped to Richmond. I believe he follows Hawthorn now. Again, who cares? He was a nippy, in-and-under player for the Panthers' junior squad, bewildering everyone with his ability to kick with both feet. In cricket, he could bat both ways too, which not only confused but thoroughly annoyed everybody. His genuine glory years unfolded in an Under 13 Panthers team, alongside a fantastic, nuggety kid called Truck Barnett. He wasn't *like* a truck; he *was* a truck. He could bust open a pack, actually burrowing under the ground with the footy, vanishing from sight. Then, he'd spring up out of the grass five or ten yards away and bang the ball fifteen or twenty yards towards the goals. He couldn't kick far, but that was never his primary value. Nobody dared go near him because he never ran around people; he ran *through* them. They were a magnificent junior team. I can't quite recall if they won a flag or not, but they certainly reached the finals. We captured Super 8 footage of Pete and Truck and all those other grommets barrelling their way through the game. Junior club footy at its absolute finest.

Dad, I'm told, had been a good, solid flanker himself. Apparently, at one point, he was invited to train down at Arden Street with North Melbourne, with a genuine chance of a run with their Seconds. For some reason, that never eventuated. He could also handle himself in a fight, having trained with a well-known trainer in South Melbourne during his cycling days there. He was a pretty successful professional rider with the South Melbourne Cycling Club in the mid-1950s, famously coming second in the Regal Wheel Race in 1954. We still have pictures of him crossing the line, half a wheel behind the winner. He earned enough that day to purchase all-new appliances for his and Mum's modest flat. There's also a picture of him slowly riding around with a huge bunch of flowers, typically presented to winners and place getters. There he is, searching for Mum, who must have been bursting with pride. She always recounted what a great rider he was. Forty years

Are You Thinking What I'm Thinking? A Patchwork Journey Through My Life... So Far

after his career ended, she was still raving about his amazing calf muscles.

Later in his career, Dad suffered a quite horrific stack on the board track at Essendon, which removed an enormous amount of skin. My enigmatic Pa, I was told, tended his wounds for weeks, looking after Dad remarkably well. After that, Dad lost his nerve—and no bloody wonder—never advancing any further in the Bike world. I cherished his riding silks for many years, but they eventually deteriorated, and we chucked them out in the end.

Dad served as runner and trainer for us in our junior footy; he and Mum drove us everywhere and fully supported our footy endeavours. They were enormously proud of us, always positive and helpful. Dad would become furious if he felt we were being badly done by or treated unfairly in any way. He was fiercely protective of us and could be quite scary when angry. Yet, he never, ever hit any of us. He was a beautiful, simple, loving, hardworking father, and I feel incredibly lucky to carry around some of his DNA.

We always had a footy with us. I remember one sunny day at the Eltham footy ground. Dad stood in the goal square, and we three boys were shouting for him to kick it. He booted a drop kick from the very end of the ten-yard square, and it went and went and went. It was the biggest kick we had ever witnessed. It landed directly in the centre of the ground. It was unbelievable... Mum nearly fell over, laughing so hard. We boys were utterly dumbfounded. Dad simply smiled and walked away—cool as you like. 'Do it again, Dad!!!' we yelled. He just smiled. 'Only the once,' he said. He couldn't possibly have done it again if he'd tried! It was a once-only event. His timing could surely never have been that perfect more than once. In his street clothes, wearing work shoes, on a sunny afternoon in Eltham, he booted that Sherrin about seventy-five metres or more. Why would he ever try again? He'd done it once! Mum could barely stand from laughing! Absolutely legendary stuff!

Are You Thinking What I'm Thinking?
A Patchwork Journey Through My Life… So Far

I was an okay footballer as a kid. I loved it, couldn't sleep before games with a mix of nerves and excitement. I played in two losing Grand Final teams: Greensborough Maroons Under 13s, and later, a strong Under 15s team at Eltham. There were some great players there, including the dual Brownlow medallist Peter Moore, and plenty of other fabulous talents. We lost the Grand Final in my final year of footy. I can't recall who we 'came second' to… though perhaps it was Templestowe, now that I ponder further. Anyway, at fifteen years of age, different paths were calling me. After so many years completely engrossed in footy, it was gradually losing its appeal on multiple levels. Things change…

In my last two years 'wearing the boots', I was fortunate enough to play under a wonderful coach, Noel Spoor. I remember watching him play for Eltham seniors; I have never witnessed a man with more sheer determination and conviction on a football field. He was actually awesome to observe, completely fearless. Not a tall man, but solid, fast, and remarkably clever. Opposing players were always wary, even a little scared of him. His fierce determination was palpable. He was one of those coaches and mentors who just commanded your respect. His presence demanded your attention. He was not merely a football coach but, to varying degrees, a life mentor to every boy on that team. His presence stayed with me for years. I'm truly grateful for the presence and lasting legacy left by Spoory. But other things were calling me…

My dear father: At the beginning of the following season, when I would have been bumped up to Under 17s level, he casually asked me, 'Are you playing this year?' I couldn't quite look at him as I murmured, 'Nah.' Then, I did glance. He gave a tiny, sharp little head nod and simply said, 'Okay.' But I could feel his disappointment. As I've said, I was an okay footballer, and he was so proud of me every time I ran out to play. Dear Dad, he always let me take the path I wanted, never trying to push me down a road I didn't want to follow. He let me be who I wanted to be. What a man. Bless him.

Are You Thinking What I'm Thinking? A Patchwork Journey Through My Life... So Far

Proof!!... that brother John is actually a Carlton supporter. Yes, despite strict firearm laws he is actually pointing a gun at the photographer, my mother, demanding she purchase him a Collingwood jumper. Evidence of the crazy, rabid nature of the Collingwood supporter. That's me standing to attention, thinking maybe umpiring is a worthwhile path to take. Brother Pete, far too cute in the front. And sister Jane, smiling, stoic, symbolically slightly sperate on the left of frame... dear ol' Dad doing the best he can and cousin (Sheriff) Leigh in the rear of the shot, about to fire up the tractor to take us for a spin!

Are You Thinking What I'm Thinking?
A Patchwork Journey Through My Life... So Far

Eltham Panthers U15 Preliminary final victors! Me, racing big Pete Moore to sign up with the VFL scout that was waiting at the back of the goal square. I tripped over Bruce Russell, just there to my left in the EHS school jumper; so Pete beat me to the signing (he was on a mission!) The rest is history; he goes on to win 2 Brownlow's. I, with a weird twist of fate, become a highly respected Banana...

Umpire Radley, about to run his first senior game, mid 1990's

Are You Thinking What I'm Thinking? A Patchwork Journey Through My Life… So Far

Ya can't act, and Ya can't umpire!

These were the words bellowed at me in the early 2000s by a rather inebriated woman, leaning over the fence at a guest umpiring appearance I made in the very heart of South Australia. For a decade, I had been an umpire for the New South Wales Australian Football League, and I loved it! Fit? Yes, I was! I could outrun most of the players… backwards! Waving my arms around with the grace of a ballerina, blowing the whistle, adjudicating the game, calling 'play on!', bouncing the ball, and talking them out of brawling – it was pure exhilaration.

There actually is no game without the umpire. When it's good, it's magnificent! You're simply there to help keep things ticking over. It's the greatest game on earth, and when you're the umpire in a close encounter, with thirty-six blokes out there running as if their very lives depend on it, you take that responsibility seriously. A wonderful era – Three Grand Finals, one hundred and ten games. I earned a bit of money, stayed as fit as a trout, and thrived on the pressure. I've still got my Acme Thunder whistle. But on this particular day…?

I was out in Leigh Creek, South Australia, filming *Rabbit Proof Fence* – another superb Aussie classic that I had managed to wrangle my way into! I've appeared in so many Oz classics; it's brilliant! It was mid-season for most footy competitions, so I enquired if there was a game I could officiate while I was there. I'd never umpired an outback match, and they're always short of officials. I made contact with the relevant league representatives, and, of course, they had a senior game for me to run on the Saturday. My running partner was a decent bloke, carrying a few extra pounds and looking a tad weary of it all, so I ended up doing most of the legwork. There were some cracking skills on display out there on that dusty oval, especially from the Aboriginal players, naturally. My goodness, they are an absolute pleasure to watch. The sheer athleticism and the effortless ease with which they perform; it's as if the ball is on a string, and they always seem to have time, so much time…

Are You Thinking What I'm Thinking?
A Patchwork Journey Through My Life... So Far

The game itself was fine, as I recall, but the folks around the fence were necking beers and Jim Beams pretty freely, and were in full voice. They had been hammering me all day. I was wearing the NSWAFL gear and, I'm sure, looked a little out of place – an easy target, no doubt. This particular woman believed I'd denied her son a free kick that was due to him near the boundary line in the right forward pocket. But no... I awarded the full forward the mark, blew time on, and jogged in to line him up for the tricky kick from the boundary. As I positioned him and cleared the area, there was a fleeting moment of silence from the small but vocal crowd. That's when she bellowed those infamous words: 'Ya can't act, and ya can't umpire!!' Ouch... For years, I'd endured all manner of abuse, been called every animal and scoundrel under the sun... but *this*? This one stung. What?! Hadn't she seen my fabulous work on *Priscilla*? *Babe 2*, *The Big Steal*, all those Cop shows... I'm B1 for Christ's sake! Surely that counts for something?!

Thankfully, the siren went not long after, allowing me to make my exit with what little dignity I had left. 'Can't act?' I returned to my accommodation, making sure I learned my lines thoroughly, just like a good classically trained umpire ready for his work on this important Australian picture! I *can* act!!!

I stuck with umpiring for a few more seasons after that, just in a semi-retired, part-time, take-it-easy sort of way. My very last game was at Campbells Creek in Central Victoria. Oh, my goodness! The ground was so rough, you wouldn't run cattle on it! I strained an Achilles in some hole about centre half-forward, at the Newstead end, in the very first bloody quarter, and I thought, 'You know what, Kenneth? This is your last game.' Ironic, really, that the oval I was running – or, more accurately, hobbling – on was the home ground and original club of the great Richmond champion, Dustin Martin... I packed up my gear after the game, limped home, and spent the rest of the night on ice treatment. A perfect finish to umpire Radley's decade with the whistle!... Play on!

Are You Thinking What I'm Thinking? A Patchwork Journey Through My Life... So Far

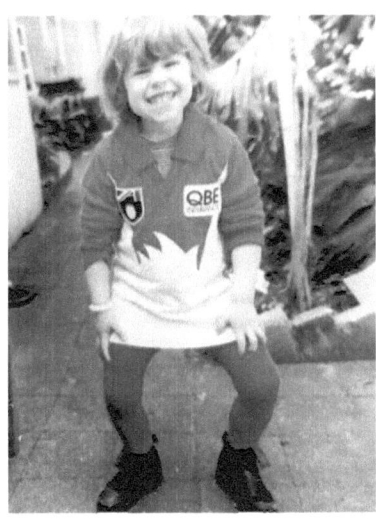

Georgia insisting I somehow sign her up with the Swans at 3 years of age. She refused to accept that AFLW was still a couple of decades away.

Holden Commodore. Bought for 10 grand from a shonky dealer on Parramatta Road in Sydney. Let's call it a learning curve. This thing gave us so much trouble over the first months and cost a fortune in repairs. Finally it ran ok. We packed it up and moved to Melbourne in December 1997 to reside at our first home purchase in Chirnside St Kingsville – a life changing move! Thank you, Bananas, for the deposit!

Yamaha TTX 115cc Scooter. I've owned this baby for less than 2 weeks! Purchased for 16,000THB (approx $700AUD) from a fabulous family in a rough little repair place not far from Bangkok Hospital in Rayong, Thailand - where I've parked myself to soak up some lovely Thai culture, eat amazing food and live the life of a writer for a while. This little Yammy rolls along just fine for me here. I've learnt to ride like a Thai person... only slower!

Are You Thinking What I'm Thinking?
A Patchwork Journey Through My Life... So Far

Yamaha TTX 110cc   Holden Commodore 1986

Ten Love!... for Gerard Kennedy

Downstairs in the basement 'sports' room of the Gunnadah RSL in the mid-1980s, I was hitting winners! Table tennis. I won ten out of eleven games. YEEEESSSS!

Gerard knew I was playing to his glass-eye side, and laughed longer and louder with every game he lost. Losing to Gerard wasn't simply losing; it was something else entirely.

A newly trained actor, just a year out of NIDA, all bushy-tailed and brimming with enthusiasm, I was enjoying a reasonably fertile period with a couple of feature films and a mini-series or two under my belt. Here I was, thrashing out some games with this genuine legend on a hot New South Wales evening, after an easy day's shooting and a pint 'n' parma. Gerard, of course, had some sort of vegetable dish. He was a devout animal lover, and having once worked in an abattoir, he hadn't touched meat since the 1950s.

We were filming *Stock Squad*, a quaint little rural Police, mystery picture starring the strikingly handsome Marty Sacks, the fabulous Kris McQuade, Gerard as the bumbling country cop, and Michael O'Neill as his sharp young offsider. I played one of the bad guys; my character's name was Pitt – I called him Doug. Doug Pitt. There were weapons and tough talk involved, naturally. Howard Ruby directed it. Howard was a delightful chap... 'Ready, set, action!' he would frequently bellow, a fabulous burst of energy, like a race starting! Ross Berryman shot it; a fabulous cinematographer. Jay Hackett was there too, along with various other Australian stalwart cast and crew. It was a marvellous time to be involved in the Australian film business – the 10BA tax incentives were providing healthy returns to film investors, there was plenty of work available for cast and crew, and we from Down Under were gaining a formidable reputation as excellent practitioners all around the world, particularly in the now rather sad and isolationist USA.

Gerard taught me so much. About cultivating a quiet, professional attitude on set, showing polite appreciation for everyone's work and personal space, and the importance of welcoming and accommodating new ideas or changes that might be thrown our way. All of it was water off a duck's back to Gerard. He had this quiet wisdom and humility about him, qualities that have always profoundly appealed to me.

At that buoyant time, I was (predictably) drawn to the wild types living out there on the edge – rule-bending cowboys brimming with what appeared to be confidence, something I didn't really possess. Then, as I got older (and perhaps wiser?), I learned that this apparent confidence was most likely a smokescreen for other things, deeper and more vulnerable than the bravado dance they were stumbling through… they were fun times, though, and that's as important as anything else.

Gerard, however, was a real man. Quiet, measured, like the old bull from the story. He had no need to impress, to dominate the room, or to insist on being the top of the actor hierarchy on set, as some fellows seem to require. He was always respectful, steady, present, and available. He hit his marks accurately, never so much as a complaint or a click of the tongue during the inevitable waiting periods for technical matters to be attended to. He would offer relevant and clever little ideas to move the drama along, save time, support the story and the other actors in the scene. There was always a ready laugh, and importantly, a quiet moment for himself just prior to 'Ready, set, action!' I loved working with people who operated in that way during my early career; it taught me to emulate that very approach – and that's

Are You Thinking What I'm Thinking?
A Patchwork Journey Through My Life... So Far

how I still work today. Standing by, a heartbeat away from being in the place I need to be, ready to launch into the scene.

Gerard did all this automatically; he simply did the work.

One memorable moment in the Police Station set on *Stock Squad*, he threw his arms in the air in a huge, guffawing response to something humorous in the story. His office chair lifted off its front wheels and tumbled backwards, flinging him onto his back on the floor. This was not a rehearsed stunt, so the camera cut, and folks rushed over to ensure he was okay. 'Did you get it?' were his very first words. No, it was N.G. (no good), as Ross wasn't ready to follow him down with the camera, and the set wasn't prepared to accommodate the unexpected stunt. There was much talk and chatter... then, set up for take two, a brief rehearsal, a cushion placed down for a soft landing, and then – bang! The action was repeated by our man, just as funny as the accidental first take. Great stuff.

At this time, Gerard was working on a huge catamaran, with the ambitious goal of sailing the world! It was one of those expansive, long-term projects that some people embark upon. I wonder where it all ended up? You see, the thing about Gerard was that nothing was really a problem. If something 'went wrong,' it wasn't really wrong; rather, it was an opening for another opportunity. It happened because it happened; now, something else would follow. We would deal with what we needed to deal with and move along – without anger or frustration, just quiet acceptance, presence, observation, and a little learning thrown in. He demonstrated and embodied that kind of philosophy. It was incredibly appealing to me, a wonderful learning moment.

Everybody loved and respected him. I was fortunate to work with him and simply spend time in his company during that short period on location in central New South Wales. It was a great time and has stayed with me forever.

Are You Thinking What I'm Thinking? A Patchwork Journey Through My Life... So Far

Gerard had a great innings, lived to a ripe old age, and made a difference to so many people's lives in myriad ways. A life well lived. Rest in peace, you gentleman.

Taxis Confused

My good friend James Roden and I became mates in the mid-1980s. We moved in the same social circles and then worked together on a classic, rollicking Australian musical in December 1985 at the Q Theatre in Penrith – *Reedy River*, by Dick Diamond. It was a Christmas show for The Q. It's the only romantic lead I ever played! With a face like mine, I don't often play lovers (a standard line of mine). The cast all played in the bush band, providing the live music on stage. Songs like: 'Click Go The Shears' and 'Lachlan Tigers'. It was a complete hit, and we had an absolute ball! Audiences were in raptures night after night. It was wonderful!

With Helen Buday in Reedy River. Q Theatre Penrith 1985

At the time, for my ever-present day job, I was working on the pick and shovel as a labourer for this, shall we call him entrepreneurial, chap named Ernie from Palm Beach. He had wrangled his way into undertaking insurance work, specifically; underpinning houses that had become unstable in Sydney's Northern Beaches area – Palm Beach, Newport, Avalon – a beautiful, very affluent part of Sydney. Ernie assembled a team of backpackers, misfits, recently released 'crims', struggling actors, and surfie-type labourers. This formed a sort

Are You Thinking What I'm Thinking?
A Patchwork Journey Through My Life… So Far

of chain gang, scrambling under these houses on ludicrously steep blocks that were, quite literally, slipping down the hill after Sydney's colossal downpours. The problem was an insufficiency of concrete piers supporting these properties, causing them simply to slide.

We, the working ants, would clamber under these places and dig holes with whatever tools we could drag in there: tiny shovels and picks, jimmy bars, and small crowbars. Sometimes, bare hands were the only option. We'd fill plastic buckets with earth and rocks, pass them along, empty them, and fill them up again. Eventually, when Ernie and his rather dubious 'engineer' mate agreed that the holes were deep and wide enough, we would somehow get concrete and metal in there – by hand! We'd then build it up and wedge it under either concrete beams or timber bearers.

He made an absolute fortune from this work… Hey! It's business! He charged whatever he could for himself and approximately $60 per hour for every man on the job. He paid us $25 per hour, as I recall. He had multiple jobs running simultaneously, employing a team of about twenty guys. It was shit work, but I desperately needed to work, and it did pay a bit. I was living in Cammeray with Trish, my wife at the time, and her two delightful young sons, Stuart and Shane.

Now, dear old James was driving cabs. He suggested I obtain a taxi licence and escape those awful, bloody trenches. That sounded rather good to me, so I trained up and, in time, acquired the licence. I temporarily put down the labouring tools and began driving for Taxis Combined, based in Glenmore Road, Paddington. My first car was a sky blue 1977 Holden HX, Cab 73. It had a bloody uncomfortable seat. This is where I really learned to drive, Sydney style: fast, efficient, sharp and safe. Left foot brake – right foot accelerator. Handling the radio and the street directory whilst navigating Sydney traffic. Steering with knees? Not a problem. Reading, anticipating the traffic, and crucially, never getting grumpy… it's only traffic. All these elements were essential for a Sydney cabbie in the 80s/90s. After a few months

Are You Thinking What I'm Thinking? A Patchwork Journey Through My Life... So Far

I was 'upgraded' to Cab 297, whose seat was even less comfortable than old faithful 73.

Cab 297. Opposite the Trumper oval grandstand. Ready for a fare.

True stories from the cabs... (all my stories are true...)

Jana

I landed a fare from Balmoral Beach to Willoughby. Hitting the arrival button, I pulled up outside a grand residence. Jana Wendt slid into the back seat. Jana was a huge television personality at this point, and had commanded record-breaking fees. Kerry Packer owned Channel 9 at the time, and Jana certainly had clout. In those days, mobile phones weren't ubiquitous, nor were laptops a common sight. Consequently, Jana was flicking through an A4 folder of notes and schedules for the taping of that night's *60 Minutes* programme, which was rating its head off for Channel 9. Jana was leading the team and spearheading all promotional and marketing efforts. The face of *60 Minutes*, she was a bona fide star. And there she was, in the back of Cab 73, the old Holden perfectly handled by Kenneth the Rad.

She sat there, her distinctive heavy eyebrows framing intense, intelligent green eyes. She exuded confidence, her deep voice and impeccable outfit completing the formidable impression. I mentioned I lived nearby (Cammeray is just one suburb away) and I knew a nice,

Are You Thinking What I'm Thinking?
A Patchwork Journey Through My Life... So Far

quiet route to Channel 9. Would she be amenable to a 'short cut?' She replied in her deep TV voice, 'Fine, a short cut is a good thing.'

I eased the cab along quieter streets, hugging the waterline. We headed down a one-way road towards Tunks Park, which bordered Cammeray and Northbridge. I'd travelled that route almost daily, living as I did in Cammeray Road, and I knew it intimately. I've always been a firm believer in the 'pleasing aspect', often opting for the scenic route so the journey itself is enjoyable. Take the nice route! Life's too short not to savour the drive; it might be the last time you ever experience it!

'Big star' Jana was in the back, flicking through her A4 folder in preparation for the show. I glanced in the mirror occasionally as we travelled, always smooth with the brakes and throttle, gentle on the corners. My passengers were always comfortable. As I eased down towards the boat launch ramp, a sudden thought struck me: 'I hope she's alright with this weird route I'm taking her.' We hadn't spoken a word. I checked the mirror again. Her large green eyes met mine in the mirror. 'I like this way,' she said.

'Yeah, so do I,' I replied.

'You're an actor aren't you.' It wasn't a question.

'Yep, that's why I'm driving a cab.'

She asked what I'd been in. I rattled off a couple of titles, including *The Big Steal* – a hugely successful Australian film of its time. I actually watched it again recently, and it holds up so well. Great acting, a charming story; Nadia Tass and David Parker did a splendid job. Bisley's hair was like a character on its own, it deserved a credit!

The *Fields of Fire* trilogy for the 9 Network came up next. She said she loved *The Big Steal* and had seen and liked *Fields of Fire*. I reminded her I'd died in a cane fire in series 3, attempting to rescue a 'knucklehead' who panicked and ran *into* the flames. Should've left him, given that he survived and 'Dave' didn't!

Are You Thinking What I'm Thinking? A Patchwork Journey Through My Life... So Far

I dropped Ms Wendt at the main entrance after the security guard glanced into the cab and gave us both a wave. She completed the Cabcharge docket and handed me a generous tip. I recall Jana had broken salary records and was on massive money at the time. It was a Network docket anyway, so... She smiled and told me she'd enjoyed the journey, wished me luck, and I wished her luck back (we all need a little luck). A charming, courteous, respectful individual. A memorable fare in Cab 73. I wonder if she ever travelled that route again to 9 from Balmoral?

Five Only...

Double shifts were tough. I did many of them. Picking up the cab at 6 am on a Saturday morning and dropping it back before 3 am on Sunday morning meant more than 20 hours sitting on your arse in a car. It demands a particular attitude and intense concentration. It was gruelling work, and there was no money in it. The driver had to pay for the use of the Cab to the owner, fork out for Gas, and then hope for lots and lots of fares. An empty cab earns no money. On the weekends, after 10 pm, almost everyone who gets in the cab is drunk. If there's a group of them, it's painful listening to them blabber their heads off in loud, alcohol-fuelled gibberish. It's like people's true personalities come out when they're pissed. There's no handbrake, no subtlety, no class, and no care for their fellow humans. They'd become loud, opinionated, combative, prone to blaming, utterly devoid of empathy, compassion, understanding, or indeed, intelligence. If they were looking for a fight or an argument, a cab driver was the perfect target, hurling their victim-based nonsense at you, and as the driver and service provider, you were simply expected to endure it. That's what I mean by attitude – the driver needs to be able to read the passenger and navigate not only the route to the destination but the madness and hubris of humans. It can be tricky, and potentially dangerous.

9:30 pm on a clear Saturday: I'd dropped off a fare towards the harbour end of Glebe Point Road and was cruising back towards the city, listening for radio calls and scanning for a street hail. A young bloke,

Are You Thinking What I'm Thinking?
A Patchwork Journey Through My Life... So Far

maybe 17 or 18, sprang out from behind a phone box and hailed me. I quickly pulled over, and he promptly jumped in the back. Suddenly, two other young lads appeared from nowhere and piled in too. I adjusted the rear-view mirror down slightly to keep an eye on them. It was a strange way to catch a cab.

'The Rocks, mate, we're going to see a bloke.'

'Sure, guys,' I said, and eased off down the road. These were rough kids with a less educated sound about them. A lot of heavy swearing and aggression in their voices. They were discussing the 'cunt' they were going to see. Going to 'get' more like. I heard one of them saying, 'Five only, five only,' as he fiddled with something in his lap. I swung around and glanced at what was going on. They had a Smith & Wesson revolver that looked like Police issue. I'd used them more than once in shows, so I recognised the look and shape. The kid also had five real bullets in his other hand. I pulled over quickly, told them I wasn't comfortable with this, and could they please get out of the cab. I felt very unsafe.

They all started talking at once – 'We don't roll cabbies, mate, that's a low act! Here, we'll pay you now, have 20 fucken bucks, keep the change, we just wanna go to The Rocks, we're not gonna fucken' roll ya, mate, you're a good bloke! Just take us!'

I mean, they had a gun in their hand, and five bullets. I was pretty sure they were loaded up on drugs too. What do you do? Stay calm, that's what.

'Listen, guys, I don't feel safe right now. You've got a gun there; how do you think I would feel?'

They told me they'd put it away. I watched them put it into a bag and asked them to leave it there, please.

'Yeah, yeah, yeah, mate, it stays in the bag!'

Alright. It was a nerve-wracking trip down to The Rocks. They got out at the bottom end, at the base of the cliff there. I slowly moved off,

Are You Thinking What I'm Thinking? A Patchwork Journey Through My Life… So Far

turned right to head up through the cutting towards the retail part of The Rocks. When I was out of sight, I floored Cab 297, screeched around to The Rocks Police Station, parked in a Police-only zone, and ran inside. There was a desk cop there, looking a little bored. I hurriedly told him the story.

'They're still there, I dropped them off a minute ago!'

This all happened about a week after a Police officer had been shot in Sydney. This guy behind the desk didn't grab a radio to get a car up there – instead, he grabbed a pad and a pen and began slowly taking down notes. I was astounded.

'Officer, they're up there now!'

'Yeah, this is the procedure, mate… now tell me what happened again…'

He wasn't going to do anything. I have no idea why. I just mumbled something about getting back to work and walked out. I checked the papers and news reports the next day. Nothing about a shooting, so… maybe I'd dreamt the whole thing?

Are You Vacant?... and a Chance for a Man to Reflect

Tropical rain, typically relentless in Sydney, was belting down. It was around 7:30 pm on a dark Saturday night.

I'd just dropped a fare at Neutral Bay wharf. The ferries are such a wonderful part of Sydney life. I turned off Kurraba Road, cruised down Hayes Street, and dropped the fare at the roundabout. I watched the bloke splash his way down towards the boarding area as the little ferry sidled up to the dock. The ferry operators (are they 'Captains'? They certainly should be!) are millimetre-perfect practitioners of a unique skill set. They manoeuvre these vessels sideways with such gentle precision, nudging into the jetty like a soft kiss. *Mwah!*

So, I was pondering how one gets a job as a ferry captain as I slowly exited the roundabout. The rain thundered down on the old red Falcon. A woman came splashing down the road towards me, waving her arms

Are You Thinking What I'm Thinking?
A Patchwork Journey Through My Life... So Far

frantically. I hadn't even put the vacant light on yet. She swung open the front door – an unusual move, as women almost invariably opt for the back seat; seasoned cab users typically position themselves behind the driver to avoid unwanted conversation with a chatty bloke. She scrambled in, soaked to the bone, and blurted, 'Are you vacant?' I confirmed I was and asked her destination. 'Anywhere, just hurry!' she whispered, immediately sliding down the seat to hide herself.

As I eased up the road, I scanned for anyone else. She asked if I could see anyone. I told her I hadn't.

'Are you okay?'

'Yes, yes,' she spluttered. 'I was on a date at that restaurant there. I didn't realise the guy was going to be a complete creep. I told him I was going to the toilet and left out the back through the kitchen. God, I'm so glad you were there!'

So, she was making a hasty, unannounced departure. I took her to a fancy apartment block on the Middle North Shore, Chatswood, I think. I wished her luck as she gratefully exited the cab. Confirmed; we all need a bit of luck. Fact! I wished we could have had a camera on the guy waiting for her at the table. How long before he got a little worried? How many times did he check his watch? Did he think she was having a health problem? How long before he asked the staff if they could check the toilet or if they had seen her? Did the staff protect her secret after seeing her flee? I wonder if he stayed and ate a reflective meal alone. It would have been a valuable exercise for him, I thought. A quiet, solo meal in a restaurant after being suddenly stood up on a rainy Sydney Saturday night – a chance for a good think, mate... A glass of wine, perhaps, and a gentle, honest self-assessment – not just of tonight, but perhaps a deeper dive. To take notes on a napkin, find a little poetry in the situation, seek some value amidst it all...

Are You Thinking What I'm Thinking? A Patchwork Journey Through My Life... So Far

The Whole World is Fucked... or is it?

One of my favourite jokes is:

How do you make God laugh? Tell him you've got plans...

When things 'go wrong', when the unexpected strikes, when *anything* at all happens – good or bad – there is only one course of action: sit with it. Be quiet. Ensure everyone's safety, of course, then simply reflect. We cannot change what has already occurred; it *has* happened. This truth applies to every single facet of life. From running out of butter for your toast, to being abandoned at a dining table in Sydney somewhere on a rainy night, to a cancer diagnosis, to the death of your friend that you never arranged to say sorry to. All the experts, all the philosophers, the therapists, the poets, the songwriters, the great thinkers tell us the same thing. This is the only moment you have, the only second. What did not happen could not have happened, because it didn't. What happened was always going to happen, because it did.

How you are about what happened or didn't happen is the only thing you have any say in at all. And here's a great thing: you can train yourself to be okay. Of course, there's religion, self-help books, astrology, pop psychology, therapists, and medication – all of which can offer support. But then there's you. And when you commit to it? It works. Tell yourself you're enjoying your life, tell yourself you will sit with this event, accept it. Then, formulate a small plan to move forward... and remind yourself that it's alright, it was meant to be, because it couldn't have been any different. Crucially, affirm that your life is good. When we convey these messages to our brain, it responds positively. It just does. I've tried it, and unsurprisingly, my life functions better, I feel better, my day unfolds more smoothly. Why? Because I say so! It's genuinely that simple; though it might be challenging to maintain constantly, it unequivocally works. I am having a fantastic day! Because I say so!

Are You Thinking What I'm Thinking?
A Patchwork Journey Through My Life... So Far

A Change of Direction

I stuck with the cabs for about four years, on and off, mixing it up with acting work as it came along. It was clean work, at least – no mud, dirt, or concrete to deal with. But it never paid enough and was often a lonely existence, behind the wheel for extended periods. Christ, I've spent a lot of my life behind a wheel! I don't mind finally... I like it. It couldn't have been any different. Because it wasn't... ha!

Then I happened to be chatting to James again. He had started work at a place in Bondi Junction called Cellarmasters Wines. This place sounded great! Outbound selling and direct marketing of wine to existing customers over the phone... He advised me to give 'em a call.

Rigorous rehearsal debate!... Nicholas, Me, (the mediator), Jeremy Scrivener (Morgan) and the ever-curious Shane McNamara (Rat in a Hat)

Cellarmasters... the wine period

So, I landed the interview. The recruitment team evidently liked me enough to offer me the training, and then, hopefully, enough casual work to navigate my perpetually precarious financial existence. The

Are You Thinking What I'm Thinking? A Patchwork Journey Through My Life… So Far

company, Cellarmasters, was co-founded by David Thomas and John Piven-Large in 1981, an idea apparently imported from England. Direct wine sales were a novel concept in Australia at the time and promptly took off like wildfire. Turnover rocketed from just $1.2 million in 1981-82 to a staggering $154 million by 1996-97. David and John eventually sold the business in 1997 to Foster's Brewing Group for an astonishing $160 million. What a remarkable story of success.

They primarily employed actors within the direct marketing department. Located on the 25th floor of the twin towers area in Bondi Junction, you'd typically find up to 25 actors working their shifts on automated call systems. Our role was to tempt existing customers with cases of wine specially selected 'for their balance and taste'. Customer data, of course, was meticulously maintained, detailing their drinking preferences and, crucially, their spending habits; this information would instantly pop up on screen the moment a call connected.

One day, it went something like this:

'Good morning, Mr Large' (I had no idea who he was, just another 'very important' customer), 'this is Kenneth from your wine club. I'm just calling a few customers today with info on some fabulous cases that we've put together. I know you generally prefer a mix of both red and white wines. Would you like to briefly hear about the cases we're offering today?'

Meanwhile, Kathleen Cameron, the manager of the outbound team, was perched on her podium. Kathleen's ears were acutely tuned to the conversations unfolding across the floor. She'd heard me utter the man's name and immediately tuned into my call. It was John Piven-Large, the quiet 'money man' owner of the company. I skillfully guided him through the specials, tempting him with both the premium wines and the more approachable 'quaffers' included in the cases. He ordered two, then asked me to put him through to the manager for a moment. I did this with a questioning look towards Kathleen, then seamlessly moved on to the next call. The Davox system we were

Are You Thinking What I'm Thinking?
A Patchwork Journey Through My Life... So Far

using at the time relentlessly threw calls at you all day, making it incredibly intense at times.

After a while, Kathleen came over to me. She explained who I'd been speaking to and, at his instruction, arranged to gift me, by way of appreciation, a magnificent bottle of 1984 Penfolds Grange. This was the flagship wine of the Penfolds label, a simply astonishing, massive red! Thank goodness I was sharp and on-point at that precise moment. I had never tried Grange before, so I was thrilled – and, naturally, I gratefully accepted the acknowledgement for a job well done. The wine was later shared with my partner, Rita, and our great friend, Robert Price, accompanied by a pizza from Oxford Street, Paddo, up at the Woollahra end. I believe it's called Marilyna's now. Without doubt, it was the best pizza going around at that time.

Life-Changing Wine...

It really was life-changing wine. Extraordinary in every way. An '84 vintage, a brilliant year for Australian reds. It was unlike any wine I had ever tasted – so profoundly deep and rich. A substantial, flavourful mouthful, boasting both robust body and subtle, lingering complexities throughout. The exquisite balance, from the moment I lifted the glass to my lips, allowing this aerated piece of history to ever-so-gently swirl into my mouth, then play on every single tastebud with sophisticated richness. See? The wine training and descriptions paid off!

This would have been 1995 I'm thinking. As we savoured the bottle. Our conversation naturally turned to the vintage year:1984. That year marked my graduation from NIDA, the Los Angeles Olympic Games, and the release of the original Macintosh computer. The Macintosh was famously launched during the Super Bowl in America with a controversial half-time commercial directed by Ridley Scott, drawing inspiration from George Orwell's novel *1984*. The computer went on sale on 24th January, priced at $2,500 (which, in today's purchasing power, would be approximately $7,515). It was also a momentous year for Australian film and television, right in the middle of the 10BA Tax incentive scheme offered by the Government to stimulate the film

Are You Thinking What I'm Thinking? A Patchwork Journey Through My Life... So Far

industry. This period saw a significant boom in work, with countless movies and series being produced.

Opening an old wine and reflecting on the year it was bottled is such a good thing to do. I recall an entire pallet loaded with magnums of 1969 Cabernet Sauvignon that had somehow found its way to the local 'bottlo' in Cammeray when we were living there in 1987/88. I think it was Wynns Coonawarra. Amazing wine, and it prompted excellent reflections on that year and that entire era. We bought several of the magnums over some weeks. Some had gone bad, some were on the turn, but some... oh, mercy... the good ones? They were simply astonishing.

On reflection, that Grange moment was probably the most significant wine moment of my life. Every blessed mouthful felt like pure gold. Thank you for that incredible gift Mr Large. It was very special. The legend lives on.

The atmosphere at Cellarmasters was always vibrant, bubbling with energy and life! With so many actors on staff, there was a constant buzz of distinct personalities. And the parties! Oh, the Christmas parties were legendary! Always fully catered, they were typically held in magnificent locations – I particularly recall a ferry trip to an island in the middle of Sydney Harbour, where we'd get absolutely smashed, devour incredible food, and laugh our stupid heads off. Those were heady times, brimming with unadulterated fun. Everyone who worked there has fabulous stories to tell about the experience.

Farewell Sydney After 15 Years

I left in 1997, when Rita, the kids, and I made the decision to relocate to Melbourne. We managed to afford the deposit on a lovely, unpretentious old weatherboard house in Kingsville (thank you, *Bananas*). It marked the beginning of a new life in the inner west of Melbourne. This move happened shortly after David and John had sold the business for that incredible sum of money. Just before Christmas that year, I received a letter from Cellarmasters. It was a hand-signed card from David Thomas himself. He had personally sent one of these to every former employee, expressing his gratitude for their individual contributions to the company. Accompanying the card was a cheque, the amount varying depending on how long each person had worked there.

The accompanying note made it clear: 'This is not wages or a bonus,' it stated. 'This is a gift in appreciation of your friendship and advice. Do not pay tax on this money. If there is any argument about that, please refer the matter to me and I will confirm this.' This astonishing man, having walked away with a huge fortune, had generously shared a substantial portion of it with every single person who had contributed to Cellarmasters' success. I had only worked there for three years part-time, and I received a $3,000 cheque as a token of his appreciation. Imagine if I'd worked there for ten years! What an extraordinary individual. He consistently treated every person with respect and remarkable generosity. This incredible gesture will stay with me forever. It stands as a powerful example of how to run a company, how to genuinely engage with colleagues, and how to foster a solid, supportive culture in whatever field you happen to be involved in.

Are You Thinking What I'm Thinking? A Patchwork Journey Through My Life... So Far

Kingsville

This inclusive, respectful culture has appeared for me multiple times in both working and learning environments throughout my life. Whether you find yourself working with a team of carpenters, in a selling situation, on a multimillion-dollar feature film, in a university or a Primary School. This is the way to engage with people. Treat them with respect, listen to them, ask them what they think, let them do their job, look after them, acknowledge their achievements and support them – Janet Holmes a Court and David Thomas style!

So thank you, Mr David Thomas, and to all the folks I was lucky enough to spend time with over the Cellarmasters era. Cheers! May many cheeky little reds with no breeding but bold pretentions regularly come your way!

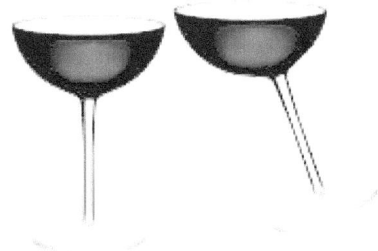

Are You Thinking What I'm Thinking?
A Patchwork Journey Through My Life... So Far

The Kiss

In my professional life, I usually play characters who punch, arrest, speak sternly, boss people around... tough, unreasonable, controlling, angry folks. In real life, I'm none of these things. 'It's acting darling'... The 'soft front and firm spine' that the great George Ogilvy (RIP) used to recommend is something I aspire to, and perhaps, very occasionally, achieve. What I'm getting at here is that I have hardly ever kissed anyone in my acting work!

The first time this rare event occurred was in 1986. I was in Western Samoa with the ABC, working on a fabulous three-part mini-series titled Tusitala – The Teller of Tales. The series chronicled the final years of Robert Louis Stevenson's life, tracing his journey from England, through Sydney, to Western Samoa. It was penned by Peter Yeldham and directed by Don Sharp. The cast was superb, featuring the late John McEnery as Stevenson, Angela Punch McGregor as his wife Fanny, alongside Dorothy Alison, Ray Barrett, Ron Haddrick, Todd Boyce, and Julie Nihill as Belle Strong. I played Belle's philandering, drinking, artist husband, Joe Strong.

What a wonderful experience shooting in Western Samoa, immersed in that thick, tropical air, punctuated by predictable afternoon rains and bright, clear, sunny mornings. It was one of my earliest experiences working for our national broadcaster, the ABC, during a period when the network was flourishing, before decades of budget cuts inflicted by various governments.

Are You Thinking What I'm Thinking? A Patchwork Journey Through My Life... So Far

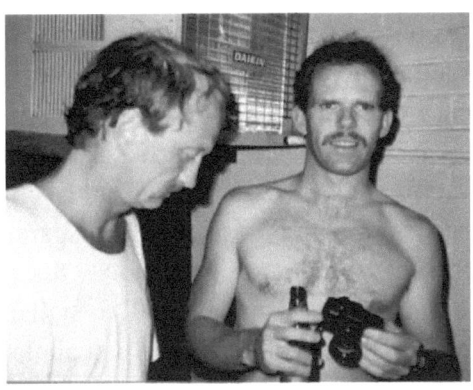

John, and the shirtless guy playing Joe Strong

No, I didn't kiss John McEnery; I'll get to the kissing bit later. I do, however, want to share one little moment I spent with him. We were at breakfast on a delightfully warm tropical morning, seated on the outdoor terrace of the resort where we were staying. Just he and I, chatting pleasantly. He spoke enthusiastically about the Cotswolds in the springtime (he was clearly loving living there at that time), while I, living in Cammeray, rambled on about the things I enjoyed and didn't enjoy about Sydney.

Our conversation drifted to the work itself – the craft of acting, performance, the concept of quiet truth, and understanding precisely what the camera might be seeing. He asked me what the largest audience I'd performed in front of might have been. I think the Parade Theatre at NIDA seated around 330 (someone can correct me there)... He then spoke of a 3,000-seater theatre where he'd performed in *Richard III*, and the sheer vocal resources required to project the needs and actions of your character to a back wall 50 metres away. He possessed a beautiful voice and was wonderfully expressive in conversation.

There was a magnetic, almost edgy quality to him, a slightly unhinged element that I've observed in some actors over the years (like Marlon Brando, Christopher Eccleston, Mel Gibson, Judy Davis, Russell Crowe, John Hargreaves, Gene Hackman... I'll think of others). It's a slightly aloof, perhaps even dangerous, quality where you don't quite

Are You Thinking What I'm Thinking?
A Patchwork Journey Through My Life... So Far

know what might come next. Tears, ambivalence, fury, or profound compassion could emanate at any moment. Directors, naturally, adore this, and the camera can certainly capture it. This particular, sparky, dangerous element cannot be manufactured; I've witnessed attempts at that too. If an actor tries to 'create' this rather charismatic trait, it can easily come across as a kind of tricksy, transparent, self-indulgent egocentricity – and the camera sees that too. Other actors loathe it. Audiences, furthermore, possess what I call a 'bullshit metre'. While most people might not have the precise vocabulary to accurately describe and explain the craft of acting, they instinctively recognise rubbishy, empty posing when they see it. They can most definitely spot a lie, signalling, indication, demonstration, signposting, or forced affectation. They might not have the words to articulate it, but it simply doesn't look or feel right, and crucially, they don't believe it.

This 'sparky thing' that I'm perhaps not describing very well, I believe, might stem from some deep well of anxiety within the actor. And every character they portray must, by extension, carry an element of that quality, precisely because it is an intrinsic part of the human playing the role. I'm certainly not qualified to diagnose this, or anything really, but I am an observer of things; I'm utterly fascinated by human behaviour. I see things, and I reflect on them. It's just what I do.

So... there's me, the young actor in his 2nd year out of NIDA. And there's John, this highly regarded, vastly experienced actor, enjoying his toast and tea. Then he asks,

Have you done much Shakespeare Kenneth?

I lamented,

No. Never professionally, I loved it at Drama school but haven't landed a role out in the world yet.

Oh you will dear boy, you will...

Then, over the toast and tea John speaks some Shakespeare.

Richard 111 (Act 5, scene 3)

Are You Thinking What I'm Thinking? A Patchwork Journey Through My Life... So Far

awaking from a dream:

Richard III: *Give me another horse: bind up my wounds.*

Have mercy, Jesu! — Soft! I did but dream.

O coward conscience, how dost thou afflict me!

The lights burn blue. It is now dead midnight.

Cold fearful drops stand on my trembling flesh.

What do I fear? Myself? There's none else by:

Richard loves Richard; that is, I am I.

Is there a murderer here? No. Yes, I am:

Then fly. What, from myself? Great reason why:

Lest I revenge. What, myself upon myself? Alack. I love myself. Wherefore? For any good That I myself have done unto myself?

O, no! alas, I rather hate myself

For hateful deeds committed by myself!

I am a villain: yet I lie. I am not.

Fool, of thyself speak well: fool, do not flatter.

My conscience hath a thousand several tongues, And every tongue brings in a several tale,

And every tale condemns me for a villain.

Perjury, perjury, in the highest degree

Murder, stem murder, in the direst degree; All several sins, all used in each degree,

Throng to the bar, crying all, Guilty! Guilty! I shall despair. There is no creature loves me; And if I die, no soul shall pity me:

Nay, wherefore should they, since that I myself Find in myself no pity to myself?

Are You Thinking What I'm Thinking?
A Patchwork Journey Through My Life... So Far

Methought the souls of all that I had murdered Came to my tent; and everyone did threat

To-morrow's vengeance on the head of Richard.

(John sips tea, crunches toast...)

My brain is thumping with, 'this is a special moment.' I am transfixed, lifted, humbled, excited, warm and calm all at once.

Thank you, I whispered.

The brilliant John McEnery

Many actors carry a monologue or two in their pocket, ready to deploy. I'm not one of them; I tend to release them after the audition, screen test, or the play itself. Yet, the quiet power of John McEnery's relationship with his material was astounding to me. Even though the words were penned some 500 years ago, they were being spoken, in that moment, as if for the very first time. They emanated from the weight and confusion of everything that had come before. The tsunami of the past had led us to this precise moment, and nothing else could have unfolded but these words – this internal argument, this profound expression of the multitudes contained within the human condition:

Are You Thinking What I'm Thinking? A Patchwork Journey Through My Life… So Far

confusion, deep regret, remorse, and self-loathing. To own, to claim, embody these words and this truth, so quietly, so intimately and assuredly, on that resort terrace on that wonderful island, with a respectful listener opposite, was as natural to this brilliant practitioner as a cup of tea and a piece of toast. I will never forget that simple, profound moment for as long as I live. RIP John.

I'd spent three amazing years studying, a period that stands as one of the great phases of my life. The hitherto unknown world of literature, storytelling, performance, poetry, and theatre had gloriously unfurled before me. It was a primary, life-changing experience that has shaped me ever since in a myriad of ways. I became honed and attuned to the written word, the subtleties of delivery, to the muscularity of language. I learnt to wrap my chops, my breath and intent around big ideas, around deep needs, to burst through obstacles. We explored the paramount importance of truth as the very foundation of all acting. Whether you're playing a Banana, a Pirate or a Street Sweeper – no matter the style, the form or the content, truth must always come first.

The excellent physical training encompassed movement, dance, gym work, mime, and clowning. And cross-dressing! Oh, yes! Over a six-week period, we explored, expressed, and created characters of the opposite gender – fabulous work! All boys, it seems, love dressing up as girls. My male acting students so often immediately reach for the frocks, nighties, hats, high-heels, wraps, and scarves during improvisations. Finally, they can shed the 'boy-boy' façade! The inner woman can break out! The 'drag classes', as we affectionately called them, were quite astonishing. Hilarious and deeply moving work was created right across the cohort (more on this later). I was a sponge, utterly soaking up everything I possibly could within this new world I was so fortunate to inhabit. What a marvellous gift to have had that opportunity.

And this specific moment with John McEnery solidified for me that I was precisely where I belonged. It served as a quiet testament to the enduring importance of theatre, performance, storytelling, and the

Are You Thinking What I'm Thinking?
A Patchwork Journey Through My Life... So Far

meticulous craft of acting. It reflects our lives back at us. It helps us observe and perhaps better understand the human condition. It grants us entry into the psyche of others, allowing us to recognise the fragility in all of us, the inherent unpredictability of life, and to observe both the similarities and subtle differences that exist between us all.

Back to the Kiss...

Now, back to the kiss... It was a lavish ballroom scene: a live band, drinks flowing, the delightful frocks, laughter, and dancing characteristic of the 1890s. We, the audience, were already privy to the troubles brewing between Stevenson's stepdaughter, Belle Strong (Julie Nihill), and her husband, Joe (me). He was in the grip of a reckless, rather lazy alcoholism, proving troublesome in various ways. He was, to put it mildly, 'under the weather' at the ball. As he threw back another drink, his eyes locked onto a beautiful young Samoan woman standing across the ballroom, out on the balcony. My task was to navigate through the dancing couples, make my way onto that balcony, my gaze never leaving hers, move directly towards her, hold her, then kiss her. My screen wife sees me, and of course, it signifies the death knell for the relationship. Very soon after, Joe is unceremoniously kicked off the island and never seen again. Good riddance to the drunken artist!

The young woman cast opposite me was the daughter of a Western Samoan diplomat. The casting team had evidently engaged in some understandable 'diplomatic' casting. This person had no prior acting experience, let alone tackling this kind of scene. Another crucial factor was that Samoa is a deeply Christian place. This sort of intimate display simply would not happen within their cultural norms. Consequently, the young woman was incredibly nervous. In those days, 'intimacy directors' were unheard of. I tried to smile and chat with her, hoping to help her relax, describing and discussing what might happen, how the shots would be set up, and so on.

With any form of physical contact in acting, there must be agreement, mutual understanding, careful rehearsal, respect, and, above all,

Are You Thinking What I'm Thinking? A Patchwork Journey Through My Life… So Far

permission. Permission from the other actor that what is about to occur is absolutely acceptable to them. There was no permission sought or given from this young woman that this gruff-looking man was going to hold and kiss her. The pretty daughter of a diplomat… there's no *acting* required from her, really; she just needs to stand there, look beautiful, and allow this drunken artist to hold and kiss her… So, I reached her, looking deeply into her eyes, leaned in to gently kiss her, and she turned her head, leaving me with a faceful of that beautiful, thick, black Samoan hair. 'CUT!' I heard called out.

The director, Don Sharp, a pleasant English chap of vast experience, came over and quietly told me he needed 'a little more passion.' Right. I was assuming he actually saw what had just happened. Take two. We went through the entire sequence again, and the exact same thing occurred. This girl was simply not going to let me kiss her. Don again had a word with me. I pulled him aside and said (sotto voce), 'Look, if I actually turn her head towards me and force her to kiss me, the whole scene takes on a different weight that the script doesn't support. Plus!' (whispering emphatically) 'Don, she does not want me to kiss her!'

We fudged the whole thing together, and I'm sure the scene worked reasonably well and supported the narrative arc of the piece. I went back to my room feeling awful. As if I wanted to be forcing some Christian girl to kiss me! Jesus! And to be told by the director that more passion was needed? No, I will not be forcing anybody, ever. In acting, we have agreement. Whether it's in intimate scenes, fighting, or any form of physical contact at all, it all becomes a carefully choreographed dance, built upon support, rehearsal, and, most importantly, agreement. I felt rather shattered and embarrassed about it. My first kiss… and it wasn't.

My second kiss, many years later, was much better! It was with Margaret Mills! Oh, what a sweetheart! And a great actor. We were working on the *Inside 2000* season at the Malthouse Theatre. The plays we performed on rotation included *Baby X, Violet Inc, Like A*

Are You Thinking What I'm Thinking?
A Patchwork Journey Through My Life... So Far

Metaphor, *So Wet and Elegy*. In one of these plays, I had a simulated, uninspiring sex scene on a couch with the brilliant Mandy McElhinney – that was fun and perfectly clunky – directed by the fabulous Tom Healey, a wonderful practitioner, hilarious chap, and joyful 'subverter of the form'.

Tom, Mandy and myself during the Inside 2000 season

My character also needed to kiss Mandy's unwell sister, a role played by Margaret Mills. I was incredibly nervous about this. Having never kissed on film or stage before, and after the previous fiasco years earlier in Samoa, I was genuinely all aflutter! Margaret, of course – a beautiful, talented, serene actor of vast experience and charm – had, naturally, done plenty of kissing in her career! I quietly confided in her that that I was nervous and asked if she would kindly guide me. We had no intimacy director, of course, so it was largely down to us. Tom, who was always mindful, diligent, and deeply respectful regarding care and, most importantly, permission and consent within the work, allowed us to collaborate on what we were both comfortable with. The kiss itself was meant to be a hot, sexy, urgent moment for the scene. Dear Margaret guided me with clarity and generosity.

Yes, we understand how such moves might work in real life; however, like all physicality on stage or in film, it is an accurately choreographed dance, built upon (simulated) truth, craft and mindfulness. We absolutely nailed this moment, thanks to Margaret's cool experience and generosity, coupled with Tom's care and trust. And yes, it worked! We achieved precisely as much connection as was needed to tell the story effectively. It was a very happy result, being guided by an expert after such a nervous start! The play itself was incredibly moving and exceptionally well-written, performed, and directed. The entire season at the Malthouse was a challenge for us all. I loved it..

I've only had one other theatre or film kiss since then! Just a quick smooch with the wonderful Rhonda Findleton, playing a prisoner who was having a liaison with his lawyer... it might have been on *City Homicide* – I've worked on so many cop shows! All of them fabulous, of course, but sometimes the titles can get a bit muddled! Ha! I love what David Mamet says about acting: 'You don't need to know the history of boxing to get in the ring and fight!' What he's really saying is, don't get bogged down with so-called preparation and research that ultimately doesn't translate to the scene or the character. Well, the same goes for all the titles and names of the fifty or so cop shows I've worked on... just get in there and do the work! With Rhonda, it was a quick kiss in the interview room! It went well, and of course, the scenes with her were fantastic. I've always admired her work; she's intense and truthful, and we worked very well together.

The chances of any more lip-smacking action in my career are slim, but you never truly know in this crazy business. It's alright, though; I'm ready! I'm an old hand now...

Dirt Blocks and Bridge Timbers

As I've confessed, my time at Eltham High School concluded rather abruptly. I wasn't invited back to complete my Matriculation – as Year 12 graduation was then known. At sixteen and a half, in late 1973, I was set free from formal schooling. Thank God, I thought. What was the point of it all? We were in the midst of a labour shortage! You could quit a job that afternoon and start another one the very next day; there was work everywhere. I knew I could even get a government allowance to go to university after a couple of years, should I choose.

Are You Thinking What I'm Thinking?
A Patchwork Journey Through My Life... So Far

The prevailing governmental policy at the time actually valued advanced education of Australians. Not a bad idea, not at all. It aimed to teach people to explore in detail, to read, to think critically, to write well, to discuss and argue ideas. It sought to foster engagement with medicine, philosophy, history, culture, psychology, design, art, engineering, the human condition, society, and politics. What a grand vision: valuing the expansion of minds and creative development.

University education remains cost-free in some of the most successful and content nations globally: Finland, Norway, Denmark, Switzerland, Iceland, Spain, Austria, and many others. Academically, these countries often find themselves streets ahead of Australia in results, boasting higher levels of societal satisfaction and a lower cost of living. A more educated general populace simply helps; it just does.

Personally, I wasn't quite ready for serious academic study then – that came much later. After completing a Bachelor of Acting at NIDA, I waited until I was sixty before working hard and completing a Master's Degree in Teaching at Monash. By then, I was very ready to immerse myself in study. NIDA, for me, was free; we were catching the very tail end of complimentary university education. Not only that, but I also received a payment from the good people of Australia to study! The Tertiary Education Assistance Scheme was drawing to a close as I pursued my studies in 1982, 1983, and 1984. I was indeed lucky. My Master's, however, cost me a hefty twenty-thousand-plus dollars, and much of that curriculum, regrettably, failed to translate directly to the classroom or adequately equip teachers with the most vital skills and strategies for navigating this often messy profession. I'll delve further into this archaic education system, which we seem stubbornly stuck with, elsewhere.

Back in 1974, my thoughts turned to a Landscaping course at Swinburne, or perhaps an apprenticeship in carpentry at some point. For the immediate future, however, I simply craved work, money, and the freedom to explore the world on my own terms. I wanted to make music and, critically, turn eighteen so I could finally get my licence.

Are You Thinking What I'm Thinking? A Patchwork Journey Through My Life... So Far

The roads of Australia were calling me. The magic age of 18 also promised legal access to pubs, the right to vote, and all the associated freedoms.

Australia, at that time, was riding the wave of a financial boom. European migration was peaking, yet the deeply ingrained and shameful White Australia policy persisted, grimly determined to keep our skins white. "NO ASIANS!! NO BLACK PEOPLE!!" the unspoken, ugly sentiment declared.

Aboriginal History: A Lingering Blight

From the initial English landing in 1788, the treatment of Aboriginal Australians remains a shameful blight on our nation and our forebears. This must be rectified. Since white settlement, the Aboriginal people of this land have endured nothing but profound disrespect and cruelty. I eagerly anticipate the welcome progress towards a treaty and appropriate representation for Aboriginal and Indigenous peoples within our system of Government.

While European and Asian migrants enriched our country with fantastic food and a strong work ethic, many Australians, generally speaking, were appallingly rude and unwelcoming to the Italians, Greeks, Yugoslavs, Dutch, English, and the few Asian individuals permitted to trickle in. Cruel, demeaning names were sadly perpetuated through generations. Yet, amidst this prejudice, culturally, we were bursting forth, expressing ourselves vibrantly in cinema, music, art, writing, and social commentary. Social mores and established truths were being vigorously challenged across our society. It was a very cool time to be a teenager.

Music was the glue that held us young folk together. There was live music in almost every pub across Melbourne. The airwaves pulsed with an incredible diversity of sounds covering so many genres.

My great friend David Brown – the hardest working man I've ever known – and I landed our first proper job. We were making mud bricks on a property out in the bush at St Andrews, a popular spot for hippies,

Are You Thinking What I'm Thinking?
A Patchwork Journey Through My Life… So Far

alternative types, artists, and anyone seeking fresh air, rolling bushland, and a life far quieter than that available in Melbourne or its more populous suburbs. Throughout the Shire of Eltham, you'd spot utes, Land Rovers, trailers, trucks, and tradies everywhere. Most of them hadn't completed official apprenticeships, weren't registered with appropriate bodies or insured to carry out the work. The vast majority learned 'on the job,' which resulted in some pretty rough work, but occasionally, something quite fabulous.

This was it: job number one. Our task involved working up a mixture of clay, topsoil, gravel, straw, and a generous dollop of cow shit with water in a large pit. Then, we'd shovel this concoction into metal moulds. Pack it down firmly, smooth off the top with the shovel, lift the mould, place it down, and fill it up again. Rinse and repeat. I think we were paid about fifty cents per brick. We'd leave the newly formed bricks lying there for several days, then turn them on their sides to encourage even drying. Once sufficiently dry, we'd carry the heavy buggers over and stack them neatly.

I swear, this is where I first damaged my back. I simply didn't know how to shovel correctly. I was using a long-handled shovel without any instruction from someone who actually understood the mechanics. Bending knees, legs apart, the precise use of muscles and bones, balance, momentum, grip in just the right places for different tasks or actions – all these crucial elements only became apparent to me as I gained more experience with hand tools. David, I remember, was far better at it than I was. He was already showing clear signs of the path his working life would take.

Are You Thinking What I'm Thinking? A Patchwork Journey Through My Life… So Far

Stacked 'muddies'… yes, they're heavy

Then I transitioned, first to builders labourer, then brickies labourer. I learned to dig a proper ditch. A very good start in manual labour. I didn't like it. Who would? But it built muscle, earned me a few bucks and taught me a lot about honest work. And I had the privilege of toiling alongside many hard-working blokes.

But one bloke, the fellow I've already mentioned, stands head and shoulders above the rest: David Haig Brown. He was, and remains, an absolute genius at this work. A veritable machine. High expectations? Yes, for both himself and his team. Strong, creative, remarkably accurate, Brownie also possesses a mind that somehow sees numbers as fluffy little clouds. He can, within seconds, calculate precisely how many bricks, how much sand, how much cement each job would require, the total cost, and a close estimation of how much time it would take. Wages, percentages, volume, area – he can crunch it all in an instant. Sharp as a tack.

Fifty years he's been at this caper, on scales both grand and humble. He's been threatening to hang up the trowel for at least 2 decades now. He won't. Still at it, perhaps a touch slower these days, but he's still the King. That's the honest truth of it. He'll probably be mortified I'm writing this. Too bad for him, because the facts are the facts.

Are You Thinking What I'm Thinking?
A Patchwork Journey Through My Life… So Far

Kenny Hughes, holding baby Angus Radley, and David Brown, 1997 Silver St Eltham

After a time, I was lucky enough to fire up on the carpentry tools. Phew… now that was much cleaner work. I landed a gig with some fabulous chippies. Chief among them were my lifelong friend, the late, great Kenneth John Hughes, and the still-going- Ron Cocks. I was a lucky boy to be working alongside these men. Excellent humans, and both incredibly clever at their craft.

I was never a natural carpenter; I'd had absolutely no prior experience with tools. As a kid, I lacked any tool-based mentoring, and my Dad wasn't exactly a 'tool man' himself. So, in these pursuits, I was a genuine beginner. Of course, Kenny didn't explicitly 'teach' anything in a formal sense. Kenny taught me heaps, through a kind of quiet osmosis. Ron too, was difficult to extract direct guidance from; he was a 'in and under' sort of nuggety, brilliant practitioner. Even today, I approach almost every job with this thought: "What would Kenny do?" I don't presume to actually know his exact methods, but what I *do* know is that he would quietly, deeply think about it. So, I always try to begin with that… just think about it. Rest in peace, you beautiful man.

Are You Thinking What I'm Thinking? A Patchwork Journey Through My Life… So Far

Kenneth John Hughes

I still love working with tools and timber. Right before the big life change in 2016 I began a little business called The Tables Are Turning, gathering old timbers, reworking and freshening them up to make into tables and pieces of furniture for family and for sale. I made three cool little coffee tables from some delightful old Australian timber. I was very happy with the progress and the idea… then indeed the tables did turn, and life went in a completely different direction.

Things change… this is perhaps the only final truth in life. Things will change.

Are You Thinking What I'm Thinking?
A Patchwork Journey Through My Life… So Far

The Tables Are Turning… some beautiful, recycled Australian hardwood. The smell, the feel of timber?… wonderful

For nearly a decade, I worked almost full-time in the building trade, shifting between various roles. Later, I continued part-time and on holidays while studying at NIDA in Sydney. Beyond that, a myriad of other jobs followed over the years. By the late 1990s, I pivoted to handyman and carpentry work, seeking the flexibility needed for acting roles. I even ran a painting business for a while in the Yarraville/Williamstown area during that period – a sensible venture, I thought. While many detest painting, I actually found a meditative quality to the work.

"Just keep going," as Brownie used to say, "just keep going." Those words have echoed in my mind, a steadfast mantra through countless flat, depressive, precipitous, and lonely moments over the years. And so far, it's always worked.

All these years on, I still possess a substantial collection: hand tools, workbenches, power tools, nail guns, clamps, straight edges, levels, shovels, picks, hammers, chisels, and more besides. They're all patiently stored at my daughter and son-in-law's place, simply waiting for the work to resume. In fact, Georgia, Simon, and I recently constructed a terrific deck together. it's a big, solid beast, built with 140 x 19mm Australian Spotted Gum decking – a beautiful, pinkish

Are You Thinking What I'm Thinking? A Patchwork Journey Through My Life... So Far

hardwood that will, I've no doubt, outlast all of us. Keep the oil up to it, and it'll stay looking magnificent for decades! "Just keep going," I remind myself, even if the pace is a little slower now. The work, it seems, simply continues.

One of these blokes is not really working

1983 BMW 4 door, 4 cylinder... and a huge turning point

I made this impulse buy from a shonky dealer in Punt Road Richmond. Nick the liar me and kids named him. Another crappy car that needed heaps of work. This reckless choice was made at a crazy time for me. It was around 2002 when a major breakup occurred in my life. My doing. I walked out on my family. Such a horrid thing to do. I cannot take it back or somehow undo the big damage I caused; I've done my very best since. Within the next 5 years there were two more wonderful children in the world; Marvin and Angelica. As complex and difficult some of the years since have been for all of us, the joy is when the four are together and with me. The fractured elements of my life make sense. Blood is thicker than water... When my four children are together, the embracing generosity and family closeness between them is a testament to each of these beautiful humans. It is all so natural and easy and fun. I'm cooking for them, they are all laughing and close... oh joy, oh wonder, oh thank you.

Are You Thinking What I'm Thinking?
A Patchwork Journey Through My Life… So Far

1983 BMW 30i

David Gulpilil

I've had the privilege of collaborating on two feature films and a television series with this giant of Australian cinema. The first of these was 'Dark Age' (1986), a film based on the Graeme Green novel 'Numunwari', which centres on an ancient, thirty-foot (nine-metre) crocodile terrorising a northern Australian coastal community. John Jarratt and Nicki Goghill took the starring roles, the late Arch Nicholson directed, Basil Appleby produced, and the delightful, Academy Award-winning Andrew Lesnie served as Director of Photography. For me, it was another great connection with a cinematographer. I played a 'Croc-Shooter', a sidekick to the villain, played by the outrageous and brilliant Max Phipps.

The film was shot at the peak of the 10BA tax incentive scheme, introduced by the government in the 1980s to stimulate the film industry. When it first launched in June 1981, 10BA allowed investors to claim a 150 per cent tax concession and pay tax on only half of any income earned from the investment. It proved an excellent way for people to park some money and support the burgeoning film industry simultaneously. At the scheme's height, films were being shot all over the country. My recollection is that, at its peak, sixty-four films were produced in Australia within a single year, though only six of those

Are You Thinking What I'm Thinking? A Patchwork Journey Through My Life… So Far

actually secured a cinematic release. So, it's fair to say some rather ordinary films emerged from that period.

Dark Age was a fairly ambitious project, primarily because it necessitated the creation of a mechanical crocodile. Minimal CGI was available back then, and digital technology was still in its infancy. The croc itself looked fantastic! It was designed to run along a track, lift its head, swivel from side to side, blink its eyes, and snap its jaws... but it did none of this. In the end, a cast of the head was made, and a diver was strategically placed underwater to raise the head and snap the jaws. The crew, quite aptly, nicknamed the film 'Croc on a Stick!' despite its technical limitations, it was a fun project to work on and has since earned its place as a 'B-classic' in Australian cinema. It never saw a cinema release and was nigh on impossible to acquire for many years. Thankfully, I now possess a copy.

My character, the croc hunter, meets a rather grisly end quite early in the film. The required death mask involved extensive prosthetic makeup, expertly crafted by a brilliant special makeup artist named Bob McCarron.

Gulpilil played a tracker, a powerful champion of the spiritual connection between croc, place, and people. I had several opportunities to meet and chat with him over the course of the shoot. What an aura he possessed – an ancient, deep presence coupled with profound wisdom. Such a handsome man too: tall, slim, with an impossibly large and generous smile. Even more impressive, however, was his precise, understated acting skill and his truly amazing dancing.

The following story, I'd wager, has at least a sixty per cent chance of being entirely accurate... which is pretty good given the passage of time and the vagaries of human recall. In one particularly exciting moment on the waters of Far North Queensland, David was in a small boat with a minimal crew, and a $200,000 Panaflex Gold 35mm film camera strapped to the bow. They were shooting the approach shot to the shore of the coastal community, gliding comfortably through the water until... the man driving backed off the throttle a little too hard.

Are You Thinking What I'm Thinking?
A Patchwork Journey Through My Life... So Far

The boat dipped deeply, and the heavy Panaflex simply plopped into the deep saltwater.

Gulpilil, without hesitation, dived in. Somehow, he managed to get beneath the camera, and with all his might, he heaved it upwards, presenting the sodden Panaflex to the crew who struggled to manoeuvre it back into the boat. They powered back to shore, where the crew meticulously pulled the entire thing apart on a huge tarp, desperately trying to save it. No luck. the camera was ruined.

A couple of days later, the 'rushes' arrived on location – that's the name for the developed film shot a day or so previously. Producers, director, designers, heads of department, crew, and occasionally us actors, would gather to watch and listen to the rushes. We all needed to see that the film was indeed being shot, that the story was unfolding. The approach shot appeared on screen, and everyone knew what was coming... we held our breath. Yes, sure enough, the angle of the shot visibly changed as the boat slowed too quickly. We saw the water rushing closer. Splash! It was in the drink... *blub, blub, blub... down we go!* Bubbles swirled past the lens for a couple of seconds. Then, astonishingly, Gulpilil's big, black hand entered the frame, fingers splayed wide, poised to grasp the camera as it sank. The motor inside the camera finally gave out at that point. But the film itself survived – celluloid being the robust material it is.

What a moment! A drama unfolding within a drama. David emerged as a kind of hero. We clapped and hooted in appreciation for his swift action.

Then, on the night of the wrap party, he danced for us. An Emu and Croc dance. It was absolutely mesmerising. Performed in wonderful makeup, with the basic accompaniment of sticks and a didgeridoo, it was an amazing experience for us all. To top it all off, in the most wonderful way, eight or ten very young Aboriginal kids joined him in the dance, mirroring the master's moves. They were committed, respectful, and precise. Oh, how we beamed and yelled! All of us, in

Are You Thinking What I'm Thinking? A Patchwork Journey Through My Life... So Far

that singular moment, felt a welcoming and profound, if small, connection to this man and his ancient culture. It was so very special.

David later played a major role in *Rabbit Proof Fence*, a film I also worked on, though our paths didn't cross during that production.

The Fencer, Rabbit Proof fence

The last credit we shared was in series 3 of the excellent American series The Leftovers. Again, we didn't cross paths – I was the captain of a ferry and David was on location in the wilds of Tasmania. He was as brilliant as ever.

David is not well now. My love and respect go to him, his family and his people.

Are You Thinking What I'm Thinking?
A Patchwork Journey Through My Life... So Far

David Gulpilil

Since writing this David has passed away. RIP

The day we told our daughter... Georgia, our first-born, was around eighteen months old, I think. It was approximately August 1995; I'd just returned from America – my first and only visit to the USA. Back in May 1995, I'd flown into Houston, Texas, with Alex Morcos, my colleague and friend, to collect our 'Best Short Film' award for The Seedling. We'd shot that film over more than a two-year period, submitting it to countless festivals worldwide. WorldFest Houston accepted the film, then notified us we'd placed either first, second, or third. I recount that story in far more detail within the 'Bill Hunter' chapter.

Not long after our glorious return, a new season of Bananas in Pyjamas was underway. Rita and I had discussed that it might be best for us to gently let Georgia know who was actually bringing the B1 suit to life. Of course, doing so inevitably challenged the validity of all the big ones: Santa, the Easter Bunny, the Tooth Fairy, God? We reasoned it was far better for us to break the news to her ourselves rather than have her hear it elsewhere.

So, we took her to the studio. We meticulously set up the moment with the costume department, a stills photographer, and the lighting crew.

Are You Thinking What I'm Thinking? A Patchwork Journey Through My Life... So Far

Rita led her onto the 'Cuddles Avenue' set in the Gore Hill Studios, and there, waiting for her, was the big fruit! She rushed over, and I scooped her up; her face was beaming with pure delight! The photographer captured the shot – which we still have, proudly framed.

Then, I squatted down as the costume folk slowly, carefully, released and raised the head of the B1 costume. Inside, I was repeating, 'It's B1, it's B1, it's B1...' then, as the head was lifted right up and taken away... 'IT'S DADDY!!!' She immediately ran to me, leaping into my arms. We both beamed, and the photographer snapped another shot – which, of course, we also have, framed. She was wearing some cool clothes I'd brought back for her from Texas, it was a fabulous moment. Of course, she's required extensive therapy over the years to fully understand and accept this trauma we put her through, but hey... life's full of illusion and disappointment, isn't it?

Are You Thinking What I'm Thinking?
A Patchwork Journey Through My Life... So Far

The big reveal for our daughter... It all worked out fine!

Eltham High School   1969/73

I lied on my NIDA entrance form. Year 12 (Matriculation/VCE?... Yes! TICK!) You see, a Year 12 qualification was a requirement, I put a big tick there. Then I crossed my fingers that they wouldn't, but If they asked questions, I'd tell them it was so long ago the records must be lost! Same process 43 years later at Monash... tick! By then it was definitely too long ago – last century!

Are You Thinking What I'm Thinking? A Patchwork Journey Through My Life... So Far

So, despite never actually completing Year 12, I now have both a Bachelor of Arts (Acting) Degree and a Master's Degree in Teaching hanging on the wall at home, confirming I somehow, somewhere, gained a semblance of academic chops. I was finally really ready to study when University came along. I simply hadn't much cared for the academic parts of secondary school. My interests then were far more consumed by girls, footy, music, motorbikes, friends, making people like me and the general practices of life discovery.

When I left Year 11 in 1973, at sixteen and a half years of age, Australia was grappling with a significant labour shortage. Workers were desperately needed across all industries. You could literally quit a job today and fire up again tomorrow in another role somewhere else. So, why bother staying at school? Why did they torture us with Shakespeare? Nobody talks like that! You couldn't understand a single, bloody word of it! (Some of the secrets of this, and so much more within the worlds of literature, theatre, art, and storytelling, would, of course, reveal themselves to me much, much later...).

I began at EHS in 1969. It was a monumental year for me. Eleven and a half years of age – far, far too young for what was to come. I was placed in 1C.

Day one, with sister Jane

Are You Thinking What I'm Thinking?
A Patchwork Journey Through My Life... So Far

What a year was 1969... The horrific war in Vietnam, The Real Thing by Russel Morris was number one for 16 weeks, John Farnham came in at number 5 with Raindrops, then number 8 with One. 119,000 people watched Richmond defeat Carlton by 25 points in the VFL Grand Final. The four biggest albums world-wide were British; Abbey Road, (The Beatles) Led Zeppelin 2, Let it Bleed, (The Rolling Stones) and Tommy (The Who). Woodstock, the 3-day festival of love, music, peace (and drugs) was held on Gasner's Farm in Woodstock USA between August 15-18 of that year.

Social change across the Western world was sweeping and profound. 'Flower power', love, peace, and freedom – a forceful rebellion against the conservative post-war social mores and expectations – was thoroughly embraced by the youth of the West. Drugs, free love, a desire to 'get back to the garden'... there were no mobile phones, no internet, and jobs were abundant.

University education in Australia was free... I'll say it again, free! Indeed, a government allowance was even provided to students to attend uni; the underlying idea was to value education for all Australians, not merely those who could afford to pay, or were willing to plunge into serious debt for it. Simultaneously, theatre, art and filmmaking were really beginning to flourish, as Australian artists

Are You Thinking What I'm Thinking? A Patchwork Journey Through My Life… So Far

began to demand their place not just on the Australian stage, but also globally – in galleries, in cinemas, and in print. It was, in so many ways, an incredibly exciting time in this country. We were in the midst of the most significant and sustained financial boom ever known, or indeed, ever likely to be known. Having 'ridden on the sheep's back' for decades after World War Two with the worldwide wool boom, another colossal beast, 'the property boom' – which remains absurdly and dangerously out of control today – was just beginning its relentless ascent. Culturally, we were making a real impact, steadfastly claiming our place as artists, commentators, researchers, and writers. A decent sort of splash, as they say, was being made in good old England. Figures like Bruce Beresford, Robert Hughes, Clive James, Germaine Greer, Barry Humphries, Arthur Boyd, and The Seekers were making significant inroads into the very country that had claimed this great southern land as its own back in 1788. 'Making it' in England was, at that time, a very, very big deal indeed.

We even had a few 'hippy' teachers at EHS. Long-hairs, alternates, and avowed lefty agitators, they subtly influenced the school. The curriculum, slowly but surely, began to adapt to a slightly more modern mindset. The wonderful Betty Burstall held court in the pottery shed, and Leslie van der Sluys developed an amazing elective course simply called 'Television, Theatre and Filming'.

Rehearsing the next big show with Debbie Webb

Are You Thinking What I'm Thinking?
A Patchwork Journey Through My Life... So Far

We had the scary Mr Adorian, an art teacher from Poland. He's the one whole ordered 'bad' boys to hold their hand out, fingers all touching and pointing up. Then, with the metal end of the big school paint brush would go WHACK, right on the tip of the fingers. I never got it, but I saw it administered. Corporal punishment was commonplace then. I don't recall if there were straps on the bottom like the previous century but there were certainly straps on hands. The cuts, they were called. I got six one day. Mr Callahan or Callagen, something like that. I forget my crime. Hands out young Radley. Both of them! When he brought the first blow down, I simply opened them and let the 14" or so thick leather strap pass between them swishing the stale air of his office. Quite a natural reaction, avoiding a sharp pain. So he gave me 7 as punishment for that. Red hands to show the classmates.

The headmaster's podium

Meanwhile, the younger teachers were reflective of the changing times. Far more casual and 'hip' than the conservative norms of the post-World War Two era, they didn't wear ties, perched on desks, used relaxed language, and infused their pedagogy with a much groovier fashion. These were also the days when 'close' relations between students and teachers often raised no more than a mere 'tsk' of the tongue. Golly, some of them would be facing gaol time now! Giving

Are You Thinking What I'm Thinking? A Patchwork Journey Through My Life... So Far

students lifts home, weekend and after-school visits for private tutoring, and specially tailored teaching and learning experiences – things were pretty loose back then.

Who could forget the day a very agitated student drove a white Holden sedan directly into the main quadrangle during class time, then proceeded to sit atop the roof, his .22 rifle resting casually by his hip, pointing skyward? My memory insists he might even have released a shot! Then, Mrs Moore, our fabulous French teacher and mother of the dual Brownlow medallist Pete (my classmate and footy comrade for a while at Eltham under 15s – yes, we actually came second in a Granny... it's only a game!), strode purposefully up to the car. Without a flicker of hesitation, she ordered, "Put that gun down!" He did. A brief chat and some stern words followed, and the entire matter dissolved rather quickly. No lockdown procedures, no highly trained, heavily armed anti-terrorist squads yet... just Mrs Moore, armed with nothing but strong, direct intent!

It was, in so many ways, an incredibly exciting time to be a teenager. Though, in Form 1, I wasn't even a teenager yet... my goodness, how I longed to be one! We couldn't really name it as exciting back then; we were all just living inside our lives. Of course there was racism, bigotry, misogyny, sexism, the sexual objectification of women, unfair workplace pay and practices, corruption, nepotism, bullying, domestic violence, and xenophobia... wait... do they all still exist in our society? Shit, maybe they do – and more! They were most certainly an undeniable part of our world then. Nonetheless, it was a vibrant, 'shifting sands of time' period, where freedom and possibility felt... well, truly possible!

The feminist movement was gaining formidable traction. Germaine Greer's seminal work, *The Female Eunuch*, became an international bestseller and a powerful catalyst for the movement. "Burn the bra" was a ubiquitous catchphrase.

AND, crucially, mobile cell phones had not yet arrived to ruin everything! People had to 'meet at the Post Office', 'be on the street corner', 'be at a place at a certain time'. People even hitch-hiked home, for goodness' sake! Hitchhikers were everywhere then – girls, boys, workers, ex-cons, schoolkids alike; they were a common sight by the side of the roads. A thumb out, a smile at the driver... and there was generally a good chance the ride would be safe. The driver had a captive audience, and the passenger secured a lift to wherever they were headed. I even hitched all the way to Bright with my great friend David Brown when we were sixteen and had just been 'released' from Form 5...

Bush Beat. Live Music Explodes Into My Life

One of my very first live music experiences was 'Bush Beat', held in the hall at Eltham High School. The name apparently changed to 'Club 70' in 1970, I guess. I know nothing of who organised it, only that hundreds of us flocked there to soak up the live music, socialise, try to score some alcohol, have a smoke, and simply be somewhere that offered a bit of action! Social media evidence (and yes, I'm calling it evidence) reveals that bands such as The Valentines (featuring Bon Scott pre-AC/DC), The Town Criers, Axiom (with Glenn Shorrock and Brian Cadd), and Doug Parkinson all graced that stage. It was electrifying. Being open to non-EHS students meant people from all corners of the Shire and beyond descended upon it. We'd already had a couple of lunchtime concerts at Eltham – Guitars were strumming, and bands were forming all over the place during this era. Music was the glue holding us all together, the soundtrack of our lives. People were expressing themselves through music everywhere. It was, and still is, so deeply appealing and mesmerising to me: the collaboration, volume, the beat, the poetry, the vibe.

If we look and listen to the music that dominated our radios and record players in 1969, the variation and quality were astonishing. You could hear the number one song of the year, The Archies playing 'Sugar Sugar', but you also had the bad-boy Stones, the amazing Beatles, and a powerful wave of blues, soul, and country pouring in from the States. Joe Cocker, Hendrix, Led Zeppelin, Free, The Who, alongside a host of incredible Aussie artists, were blasting through the airwaves on little AM radios – stereo had only been around for a short while, and FM radio was still years away. The sound quality was, by today's standards, truly crap, but we didn't know that! It felt absolutely wonderful! Music was quite literally exploding all over the world. Albums were selling in the millions; there was no streaming or pirating yet, so it was genuinely possible for musos to make some decent money from record sales.

Bush Beat felt like a profound confirmation, a guiding light for what I wanted to pursue in terms of artistic expression. I wanted to play in a band. "What can a poor boy do? But to sing for a rock 'n' roll band."

The Susan Street Incident

One night, after the show had wrapped, my friend David Meyers and I were walking up Susan Street in Eltham. Two 'hotted up' cars slowly rumbled past us; they then stopped abruptly next to a bunch of guys who were also wandering home. About ten 'Burra boys' (hoods from Greensborough) leapt out of the cars and proceeded to punch the living shit out of these lads. I immediately bolted, scrambling into the bush on the edge of the road in terror. David Meyers, who was smaller than me, incredibly, kept walking towards the melee. He actually walked *through* the punches, kicks, swearing, and cursing, calmly announcing, "I'm too young for this fellas, I'm too young for this!" And astonishingly, he didn't get hit. After finishing their 'heroic' act, the attackers filed back into their cars, which then screeched off down the road.

They had been using knuckle dusters on these lads. An engineered piece of metal hardware worn on your fist, designed to inflict a frighteningly powerful blow when you punch someone. It was an incredibly cowardly act, the whole thing. Young men were unconscious, blood was everywhere, and the air was filled with their moaning and pain. It was all quite worrying for me…

Are You Thinking What I'm Thinking?
A Patchwork Journey Through My Life… So Far

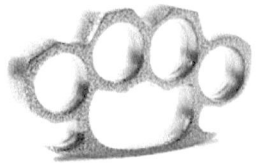

The vicious knuckle duster

(*digression to a terrifying, significant event some time earlier*)

I reckon I was in Grade Six. A few other local kids and I were on Research Park when a local thug – I won't name him; he's been dead for years now, drank himself to death, and frankly, I wasn't sad to hear it – punched into me. We were just trying to play a game of cricket on the oval. It might have been Christmas Day, or thereabouts, in '67 or '68. A brand-new cricket set had been laid out on the concrete pitch in the middle of Research Oval. I think it was just after lunchtime. Then, a slightly 'hotted up' Mini Minor came roaring up the rough dirt track, kicking up plumes of dust. Its doors slammed open, and four thoroughly inebriated dickheads stumbled out. The 'perp' (Polics slang for perpetrator – I've played dozens of coppers) would've been about 16 at the time.

He spotted the two girls with us and began staggering across the oval, lurching vaguely in our direction. The air immediately thickened with menace. Of course, he didn't like the look of me. I've always, for some inexplicable reason, been a bit of a magnet for brainless dickheads looking for a blue.

Throughout my teenage years, my twenties, and even into my thirties, I seemed to continually attract random knuckleheads intent on a scrap. It happened more times than I care to count. I reckon it's my face… a rough headed, stern looking, red-headed bloke. The kind of face that should be punched? Surely not! My default expression, or 'resting face' often looks like I'm spoiling for a fight, or perpetually angry, or something equally confrontational – and whether I like it or not, it

Are You Thinking What I'm Thinking? A Patchwork Journey Through My Life... So Far

consistently rubs some people up the wrong way. Almost always, it's the dim-wits with something to prove.

I suppose I was just staring at this goofball, who was tripping over his own tongue with the simplest of sentences. He slurred at me, "Piss off!" Then, "Where's those two sheilas I saw?" He was stumbling around looking for my sister and young Carol from next door. Everyone froze. Big Pete from next door was there, along with my brother John (who actually knew how to handle himself in a blue), and the younger kids.

The clown wheeled around again, his rolling eyes fixing on me once more. I remained frozen in a kind of bewildered wonderment – it was the very first time I'd witnessed such raw, drunken aggression up close. "I thought I told you to piss off!" he sprayed, spittle flying. Then he grabbed me, unceremoniously hauling me to the ground. On my hands and knees, I curled up, desperately trying to shield my head from the blows that began raining down. Big Pete Whitworth and my brother John finally hauled him off me. John, ever the protector, barked at me: "RUN, KEN!"

And so, I bolted.

Home! burst through the door, collapsed onto the couch, and began uncontrollably shaking and crying. My mother, a nurse's aide, was immediately, profoundly concerned. She turned to whoever else was there and announced, "He's in shock, get sweet tea and a blanket." I wouldn't, or perhaps *couldn't*, tell her what had happened... until finally, I did.

My mother was a complex creature for sure, and she possessed a formidable power within her; she had this particular way of rising up, that was both unusual, and at times, scary to behold. She rose, and announced in her ominous, decisive way, "RIGHT!" Then, with grim purpose, she began to march out through the old fly-wire door. Reflecting on it now, and given I have four wonderful children whom I would protect with my very life, I truly believe, my God, she would have torn him apart. I was so terrified, I begged her not to go. "please

Are You Thinking What I'm Thinking?
A Patchwork Journey Through My Life... So Far

don't Mum," I pleaded, "he'll get you too!" She somehow managed to stop herself, grabbed the phone, and either rang the Eltham Police or called Arthur Trayner directly.

Second Constable Arthur Trayner was the local cop who lived nearby. He actually used to work Saturdays with Dad on the Brinkcotter Chook Farm, shovelling chook poo into bags for sale as fertiliser. It seemed like only minutes later that the light blue Ford Falcon – the standard Victoria Police vehicle in those days – came roaring up Story Avenue, single blue light spinning.

A Victorian cop car of the era

I later heard Arthur apprehended the culprit, a bloke well-known to the constabulary. I don't know the precise details of what transpired up at Research Park, but I strongly suspect that idiot received his just deserts. It was old-fashioned police work at its finest. Arthur was precisely the man to dispense it – fairly and justly, as the situation demanded. No need to trouble the court system with such a clear-cut case.

I harboured a genuine fear of that brainless scumbag right up until alcohol had so completely gripped and decimated him that I knew he was entirely harmless. Someone once told me he'd proclaimed in the bar at the Eltham pub, "I can sink forty pots!" What a profoundly sad, pathetic claim to fame. These days, the pub would lose its licence for serving such a poisonous amount of alcohol to a single patron.

A couple of weeks after the incident, he approached me at the Eltham pool, the 'Frog pond', we used to call it. I froze, just as I had before. He mumbled, "Tell your Mum I'm sorry for what happened, I was drunk and didn't know what I was doin'." I simply nodded, unable to speak. His eyes were wild, unhinged. And now, he's long dead – just a story I tell.

The Art of the Stunt Fight

I've portrayed a plethora of tough blokes in films, throwing punches meticulously guided by brilliant, highly experienced stunties. I've always relished the athleticism and inherent safety involved in those moments. Pretending to be embroiled in a brawl is, I assure you, infinitely preferable to actually being in one – though perhaps not for some people, who genuinely prefer the real thing. Not me; I'm quite content with all the acting. Then, someone invariably yells **'CUT!'**, we all share a cup of tea, and patiently await the call for 'wrap'.

The truth is, I've never in my entire life, thrown a punch in anger. Some folks contend that this isn't ideal. They argue that a 'real man' knows how to fight, how to inflict damage, how to be physically dangerous. The *true* power of his masculinity, they suggest, lies then in knowing how to control that possibility, that potential – much in the way that proficient Martial Arts practitioners do. While they possess the capacity to inflict severe harm, a fundamental aspect of their training involves cultivating calmness, stillness, and the ability to assess and de-escalate situations. They seek peaceful resolution within conflict, only resorting to their martial arts discipline when absolutely no other recourse remains.

Perhaps *that* is part of being a man… and it's a philosophy I genuinely admire. Perhaps learning to fight and inflict damage would indeed have been a useful skill for me. Yet, it never happened. Instead, I suppose I largely learned to communicate my way out of trouble. I

Are You Thinking What I'm Thinking?
A Patchwork Journey Through My Life... So Far

was, and have always been, genuinely scared of violence. While I certainly harboured a temper that could flare from time to time throughout my life, a rather deep darkness that could occasionally flood me, it never, to my recollection, exploded into rage-filled action.

A boy, his guitar and dog... a lover not a fighter

I often laid on my bed on my back, in quiet stillness. I still do. Just staring at the ceiling; simply quiet, listening to the ambient sounds of the day. "No wonder," my therapist once told me, you must have been exhausted, given all the energy expended on making people like you!"

I was certainly not studious during High School. My concentration levels were limited, and I quietly but consistently felt thick headed and adrift in academic subjects like Maths, Science, Biology, and Chemistry. English? Yes, that subject, at least, held my interest. But it was in the elective, Television, Theatre & Filming, conceived by Mr Leslie van Der Sluys, that I truly found my calling. We shot films, devised plays, explored photography, delved into storytelling, and even produced mock news programmes and magazines – precisely the sorts of things one explores in Media Studies today. This,

Are You Thinking What I'm Thinking? A Patchwork Journey Through My Life... So Far

unmistakably, was where I belonged: in the creative space. My brain simply wasn't attuned to patterns, numbers, trick questions, or indeed, abstract thinking. I would clam up entirely whenever these concepts entered my orbit.

My strong feeling is that perhaps my brain simply doesn't operate easily in these areas, and that my confidence and overall development were unfortunately stunted at a very early age due to a confluence of factors: starting school a full year before I was actually ready; not being guided and taught in the specific ways I needed to facilitate effective learning; and, crucially, being rather consumed by the unstable, indeed unhealthy emotional environment I found myself immersed in. Those nagging questions, always swirling: *Did Mummy really love me? Why was I so unsure about that? Why did it feel like such an enormous deal to me? Why did they fight all the time?* And the residue of the ever-present unanswered chilling question in this boys life... *Where is my sister? Am I next?*

These days, students are meticulously observed; individually and in intricate detail. There's so much more variation and scope to accommodate diverse learning styles and paces. Such provisions simply didn't exist in that manner when I was a kid. We were all merely lumped together, subjected to antiquated pedagogical methods. The prevailing mantra was: "This is how we do it, young Radley, you can either join in or fall behind." For me, it was, more often than not, the latter. The best course of action was to hide, to figure out other ways to navigate development, ways that I actually *could* grasp! And I did. I learned to cope, and to dance around life's challenges in other ways... quite literally.

Are You Thinking What I'm Thinking?
A Patchwork Journey Through My Life... So Far

Holden Captiva 2007

I'd spent about a year studying 'ethical' real estate practices – the Jenman system – at night, while working by day on the carpentry tools alongside Gazz (Gary Dyson) and the team. This particular real estate mob spruiked a significant point of difference from standard, shonky practices. Did they deliver? I'm genuinely not sure, as I never actually worked in a Jenman office. They were so few and far between that getting a gig there seemed an insurmountable task.

I was simply looking for a regular job – I'm hesitant to use the word 'honest'. The idea of getting off the tools, donning a suit, and embracing the thrill of listing properties really appealed to me. I relished the thought of nurturing client relationships, the theatre of the auction, the cut and thrust of negotiation, and ultimately, securing a 'fair' price. Australia, particularly Sydney and Melbourne, had been in the throes of a steady real estate boom for literally decades. I had a passion for design, building, a knack for talking, and enjoyed the freedom of driving from property to property – essentially, all aspects of the industry clicked with me!

No longer needing the work truck, I traded in the Musso I'd been driving with Brad at Poyser Holden in Bendigo. He sorted me out with a black Captiva. A seven-seater, it was perfect for the kids and the occasional guest. It was a well-designed unit, with plush leather seats, a decent sound system, and a video system for the kids – a godsend on our massive journeys every second weekend and during half the school holidays for access. It all seemed like a brilliant idea at the time!

There'd been another relationship bust-up, which, with the benefit of hindsight and years of therapy, was always on the cards. Consequently, I was bereft of property, Super, and cash – pretty typical for blokes after one split, let alone two! But at least I had the car, which I was attempting, with varying degrees of success, to pay off.

Real estate, despite my absolute best efforts, didn't quite pan out. I worked my butt off, but the Global Financial Crisis hit in 2008 –

Are You Thinking What I'm Thinking? A Patchwork Journey Through My Life... So Far

virtually the day I started at Jas Stephens Real Estate in Yarraville. The subsequent three years proved tricky for countless people; frankly, nobody wanted to sell or buy property. Despite the professional challenges. I loved living in Williamstown during that period (2008-2011) and still hold such warm memories of my little apartment on Victoria Avenue, a mere 150 metres from the beach. I cherished the times the kids stayed, and loved the vibrant atmosphere down there. The Captiva served me faithfully until I eventually offloaded it around 2015.

Holden Captiva 2007

The Oils. Melbourne Cup Day – sometime in the 90s.

Midnight Oil were deep in rehearsal in one studio at ABC Gore Hill, the very same complex where we filmed all of *Bananas*. We, the *Bananas* crew, were rehearsing in the other. As the lead-up to the big race approached, around 2:30 PM, I reckon, we'd already laid out an impressive spread of nibbles and bubbles. I seem to recall some rather fetching hats were involved, though whether we organised a sweep is lost to the mists of time.

Are You Thinking What I'm Thinking?
A Patchwork Journey Through My Life... So Far

It felt only right, a bit rude even, not to invite the Oils in for a celebratory glass of bubbles and a graze on some crackers and cheese while we watched the race that stops a nation on a monitor wheeled in on a trolley. The *Bananas* floor manager, who I'm pretty sure was Ian Cicciari, gave a knock on the Oils' studio door and extended the invitation.

So, in they tramped: the sweaty Oils and the relatively clean, dry Bananas – rehearsal wasn't exactly where our sweat happened. We offered the band some champers or a beer, but to our surprise, they opted for water. And so, the party-ready Bananas were knocking back the bubbles and beer in full Melbourne Cup party mode, just a bunch of good-time fruit ready to rock the house! Meanwhile, the boring, conservative Oils were sticking to water like good boys. Rock on Bananas!

An elevated Banana in rehearsal

Are You Thinking What I'm Thinking? A Patchwork Journey Through My Life... So Far

Johnny Depp

Pirates of the Caribbean: Dead Men Tell No Tales is, without a shadow of a doubt, the biggest budget picture I've ever had the pleasure of working on. Months before, I'd actually auditioned for the role that ultimately went to David Wenham. But then, they circled back with an offer to test for a new character, one that had been resurrected from Walt Disney's original concept for the story: Pig Kelly.

Pig Kelly – a big, robust pirate with a rich history and a formidable reputation. It's a cracker of a sequence, and I was chuffed to bits to be offered the part. This was an actual acting moment in the story, not just explosions, deafening noise, and hundreds of actors milling about. In the scene, Jack Sparrow has a rope cinched around his neck, tethered to the towering skeleton of a long-dead whale. Sparrow, naturally, owes Pig a fair whack of money. Since he can't pay, Pig, as a default, makes him marry "my poor widowed sister... she's been looking for an honest man, but you'll have to do." She's hardly the most attractive creature to ever draw breath, and, of course, Sparrow's a bit reluctant. Pig, ever the charmer, holds a gun to his head and snarls, "Say I do, or I'll put a bullet in your skull." High stakes indeed for dear old Jack!

It's a fantastic sequence that took two full days to shoot on location on the Gold Coast, Queensland. This was a pretty substantial moment for me, considering the film's budget, the status of my character, and, of course, working opposite one of the biggest 'stars' in the world. I had three trips to the studio in the weeks leading up to the shoot for makeup and wardrobe tests. Penny Rose, the multi-award-winning costume designer, was an absolute riot – OMG, what a character! In the Pirates' story, it's quite a pivotal moment, a turning point for Jack.

Just a quick note on Johnny Depp's demeanour and general professionalism. So many of my students invariably ask me, "What's he like, Sir?" A mere whiff or sniff of fame and celebrity is so intoxicating to young folk in our commercial, Western culture. What I always tell them is this: "I'm very happy to report he's a gentleman. One hundred per cent professional and kind to the cast, crew, and his

Are You Thinking What I'm Thinking?
A Patchwork Journey Through My Life... So Far

fans." People are always genuinely pleased to hear me say this. "Yes, I thought he would be," they'll often respond!

I suppose it would be incredibly easy, after many years of being treated like some sort of god, to actually *believe* you are some kind of deity. I've worked with boring Hollywood types who are so wrapped up in this silly status thing that I'm sure, in the end, it does absolutely nothing for their personal well-being or their mental health, let alone the effect it has on the unfortunate cast and crew working with and around them. This bloke, Johnny, is quiet and kind to those around him, speaking with respect and care to everyone. He shows genuine compassion; he even visited the cancer ward of the Brisbane Children's Hospital while I was there, in costume, of course.

The first day of shooting was a fourteen-hour day, with the cameras fixed on JD all day long. There was plenty of intricate choreography, lots of logistical challenges to consider and manage throughout the day. He was 'on' for the entire day. He never lost his cool, never got annoyed, was always mindful and professional, and forever inventive. We worked really well in the scene, bouncing off each other, ad-libbing – just working, like we do. I mean, it's what you'd expect from anyone in this line of work. But when the work is buoyant and inventive, it's always affirming somehow.

We didn't actually get to my shots that day. The cameras were about to be turned around onto me, but then the tropical rain hit. So, my makeup had to be removed. It was a big, four-hour makeup job for me, and it probably took about forty-five minutes to gently take it all off.

Then, upon leaving the set, the driver taking me back to the hotel rounded a corner leading out to the highway. The road was half-closed. Hundreds of people were there with security, police, and barriers. "What's all this?" I asked the driver. "Oh, they're waiting for Johnny," he replied. "He comes out and hangs with the fans for a couple of hours after wrap on most days. He does selfies, chats, says hi…"

"Shit," I thought. "He's just worked fourteen hours, and now he's coming out to meet and greet the fans for another two?"

Are You Thinking What I'm Thinking? A Patchwork Journey Through My Life… So Far

I spoke to him about it the next day. "Yeah, I do that," he said. "It's the only chance I get to say thank you. These people go out of their way to support me. It's the least I can do…"

My part of the scene was scheduled for the end of the second day. Johnny had been off set for a couple of hours. There were two other exact lookalikes of Jack Sparrow on set every day, all day long. One to set lighting and props, the other bloke was his stunt double and had been working with Johnny for ages. Seriously, these cats are identical to JD! What some Hollywood people do (a shocking practice) is get the stand-in or the stunty to read opposite the other actor in the scene when the camera isn't on them. It's a bloody awful way to work.

At this moment, Johnny wasn't actually on set… *mmmm*. Then, I looked up the hill. Who was wandering down that hill, ready to work? Of course, our man himself. So, we did. We worked. Multiple cameras were fixed on me for three or four hours to bring the scene home from Pig Kelly's perspective. Just like we do, just like we should, Johnny was opposite me, putting in one hundred per cent to the work, supporting, inventing, challenging, creating for the full four hours. Not one camera was on him.

I shouldn't even need to mention this, really, I know. However, the whole 'major star' thing means that I *do* want to mention it. He's a gentleman, and I absolutely respect him.

"Did you get his number, Sir?" The kids always ask me… "Well, he wanted to swap numbers, but I said, 'Johnny, let's just keep it professional, okay?'"

"Whaaaat? You didn't get his number??"

"No, now let's get back to work… open your books to page ten…" "Wait!… Really, Sir?…" "Shush, let's look at the Black Plague in Europe…" Teens, eh? Fame means so much to them!

At the very end, when 'final cut' had been called, I held out my hand and said thank you to JD. He ignored my hand and came in for a huge, strong, blokey kind of embrace, looked me straight in the eye, and said,

Are You Thinking What I'm Thinking?
A Patchwork Journey Through My Life... So Far

"Will you believe me that the pleasure was all mine? You were fucking brilliant!"

"Awww... thanks, man." He then went off to meet his fans, then home to his two little hounds and his current wife. I headed back to the hotel for a solo, reflective bourbon and planned for the journey home the next day. Another moment complete on the cinematic pathway... always thankful for the work... always quietly looking forward to the next one.

Onward!

Pig Kelly, The Preacher, Jack Sparrow and a crewman. Pirates of The Caribbean, Dead Men Tell No Tales

Mitsubishi Triton Twin Cab.

I had moved back to Castlemaine in a live-in situation with a local woman and her 5 kids (yes) in mid-2011. I set to work renovating her home. The Captiva wasn't ideal, but we made do towing the trailer and gently using it as a kind of work truck. After getting rid of it I used the very last of my Super to buy a good quality real work truck – The Triton. It was a tool, a necessity for the work. Back on the tools! Trying to handyman my way around the place. It kind of worked, in the humblest of ways. So, that relationship ended after 7 years. Again, hindsight and reflection tells me this was always going to happen... years of reflection and thank goodness – excellent therapy with a brilliant clinical psychologist finally helped me make some sense, gather some understanding of this pattern.

Are You Thinking What I'm Thinking? A Patchwork Journey Through My Life... So Far

Of course going to NIDA and exploring; through stories, performance, poetry and theatre the depth and wonder of what it is to be human fitted perfectly with the questions I was asking over this time. How can a disagreement and an attachment to certainty lead to World War? What drives ambition, revenge, valour, honour, bravery, cowardice... how can people fall in love? Out of love? Important questions of life. But Kenneth, It's nice that you, with the help of 500 years of work on the text of Macbeth can unpack Will Shakespeare's deep observations of the human condition but can you satisfactorily answer these questions in the context of YOUR life mate? The answer for so long was no. Trapped in the miasma with insufficient tools and guidance to garner reasonable understanding. But then, the expert attention paid by my highly skilled and professional therapist over an extended period helped guide me towards deeper reflection and a critical exploration of my life patterns... understanding is a great start.

Mitsubishi Triton 2018 Twin Cab

Trumper Oval

Nestled sweetly in Sydney's fabulous inner eastern suburbs, right on the edge of Trumper Park, bordered by Glenmore Road, Roylston Street, and Hampden Road in Paddington, sits a delightful cricket/football oval. For me, it absolutely brims with memories. It's named after Victor Trumper, widely regarded as the 'most versatile and stylish batsman from the golden age of cricket.' Born and bred in

Are You Thinking What I'm Thinking?
A Patchwork Journey Through My Life… So Far

Darlinghurst, he sadly passed away in 1915 at just 37 from what was then known as Bright's disease – an archaic term for Nephritis, a condition where the kidneys, compromised by infection, genetics, or other factors, fail to filter blood correctly.

Originally christened Hampden Park, the oval was built on a reclaimed swamp, in a very low-lying area of Paddington. Both the peaceful, bird-filled park and the oval were renamed in 1931 to honour the great batsman, who'd represented Australia in 48 Test matches between 1899 and 1911. He also toured England four times with the Australian team. Can you imagine those six-week journeys to and from England, four times over those years? I often wonder what those long, slow voyages were truly like for those players.

I lived in a tiny cottage at 11 Roylston Street with Rita, my partner at the time. It was right next door to George and Greg's panel beating shop – they owned the place and were happy to have us there for a few years, from about 1992 to '97. It was a rough, character-filled cottage with a brick path leading to the garage out the back, which we'd converted into a kind of bedroom area. Both our kids, Georgia and Angus, were born there, in 1993 and 1996 respectively, in what are now gentrified townhouses but was then the Royal Women's Hospital, Paddington, just up the road.

The Taxis Combined (Taxis Confused we called them) base was very close – a decent torpedo punt away, on the corner of Hampden and Glenmore. A short stroll past the Trumper Oval grandstand to pick up the Cab. I've said a bit about the Cab era – But, it taught me a lot about the geography of greater Sydney and honed the driving skills… very useful for a fuel user like myself.

I learned a lot about navigating Sydney during that period, and my driving skills improved enormously. Reading the traffic, understanding road conditions, taking the best line through corners, braking and accelerating smoothly and at the correct times, learning not to get annoyed with traffic (it's *only* traffic!) – and, importantly, I taught myself the left-foot braking technique. The left foot hovers over

Are You Thinking What I'm Thinking? A Patchwork Journey Through My Life... So Far

the brake, which significantly reduces reaction time on busy roads. The left, right, left, right method works incredibly well in every way, especially in fast-moving Sydney traffic on narrow roads with skinny lanes and with people always in a hurry! There's more to say about the cabs, but for now, back to Trumper.

Plenty of notable things happened on Trumper Oval over those years. I even saw the great West Indian player Malcolm Marshall bowl on the pitch. I'm not sure why he happened to be playing there, but *OMG* could he bowl! Next-level skills, that! How the hell could the batsman even see the ball, it was travelling so fast – and then it would move sideways through the air as if some magic had taken hold of it.

The cricket pitch and the general maintenance of the oval were in the hands of a local council worker called Ted. 'Hanoi Ted', I called him. He was originally a Kiwi. His Australian Indigenous wife, who never spoke, and their little kid used to sit in his tiny shed/office area all day long as he moved about doing his tasks. I don't know where I heard that he'd served in the American war in Vietnam. For which defence force, I also have no idea. New Zealand *did* send about 3,500 troops to Vietnam between 1964 and 1972, so maybe he served in the Kiwi forces. I was told he was from some sort of special, elite force that actually parachuted into Hanoi during the war. He was a weird little bloke who moved like a robot, driving his mower around and taking the roller to the grass pitch with great care. He always waved hello. Though, I heard him yelling furiously at his diminutive wife more than once.

He meticulously marked out the creases and watered everything as needed. When cricket season finished, he'd mark the boundary line, the 50-metre lines, the centre square, and the centre circle, ready for the Australian Rules Football season. The oval was the home ground for the East Sydney Australian Rules Football Club – 'The Bulldogs' – wearing the old Footscray colours. Part of the NSWAFL. Hanoi Ted... I wonder where he is now?

Are You Thinking What I'm Thinking?
A Patchwork Journey Through My Life… So Far

I umpired quite a few games on this neat little oval. I ran for ten seasons in total, probably six or seven of those for the NSWAFL Umpires Association. I chalked up 110 games in total and officiated in three Grand Finals. It was a great period for my fitness. They paid a little bit, and it was good to be close to the game, carrying the responsibility of umpiring – it was especially great during the two-umpire system, as there was a teamwork aspect with the other field umpire that was really satisfying to be involved with.

You could see my cottage from the ground, so I used to sneak out of the house with my tie on (part of the dress code for umpires), kit bag slung over my shoulder, and walk around the back of the ground to enter. I didn't want the visiting team to know where I lived. The Easts boys knew, but umpires need to be careful. "Always park close to the entrance. And make sure to reverse in for a quick getaway." If things got unruly or angry at the end of the game, or if you weren't liked by someone, it was a sound idea to be able to escape quickly. I was followed to my car once at a game out in the west of Sydney by this very scary player who wasn't happy with my officiating. "You think you're smart, don't ya!" he snarled, getting closer and closer. He wasn't the brightest of shining lights, and I remember he'd been crass and thuggish during the game. I was glad to jump in the getaway car and beat it back to the trendy Eastern Suburbs.

Unsettling Encounters and the Call to 000

I found a dead man next to the grandstand at Trumper. There was an old bloke who used to shuffle around the oval just before dawn. I'd see him at 5:30 AM on my way over to pick up a cab for the day. He always had his tiny little white mutt of a dog running around with him, always rhythmically huffing as he shuffled along in the early morning pre-light. Well, one morning he was flat on his back at the foot of the grandstand, arms bent up next to his chest, his dog nowhere to be seen. His eyes were slightly open with a surprised look about them. The top part of his legs and face were very pale, while the bottom part had a kind of bluish hue. I felt for a pulse, but I knew he was gone. A police

Are You Thinking What I'm Thinking? A Patchwork Journey Through My Life... So Far

officer friend of mine later said, "Yeah, when they're dead, they look dead." I called 000 and waited for the constabulary to arrive.

There was a lot of heroin on the streets of Sydney at this time. I even helped a junkie who was overdosing at the Grandstand one Wednesday afternoon. I was at home and heard frantic screaming. I raced over, and a haggard-looking young woman, clearly in the grip of a heroin addiction, was running around screeching as her equally sad friend convulsed on the ground. This woman had turned blue and was in a very bad way. I bent down to her when her friend yelled at me not to give her mouth-to-mouth! "Oh, okay," I thought. I rolled the woman into the coma position, and her friend yelled, "Don't touch her blood!" Christ! I thought. I grabbed my mobile and called 000. "Hi, it's me again!"

Thankfully, the ambos arrived really quickly. I backed off when they approached. They immediately slammed a dose of Narcan into the patient, who almost instantly sat up and started yelling at the ambos for "fucking up her hit." So tricky for the ambos! Addiction is shocking for all concerned, but I've got to say, I'd prefer to be confronted by a heroin junkie than a crack head or a meth maniac. Smack is an opioid and usually makes them soft and gentle, unless they're desperate for a hit. But crack and meth? Evil stuff. Makes them so violent and crazy. Give me a strong coffee in the morning, a Bourbon at cocktail hour, and a glass of red with the meal. I'm happy to glide through that trilogy of stimuli; it suits me just fine!

I called 000 another time when someone was trying to break into the front door at stupid o'clock in the morning. Jesus, it was scary. Scratching away and using some sort of tools to try and lever the door open. I awoke from a deep sleep to these noises; I thought I was dreaming at first. I whispered to the 000 operator that they were breaking in, right now! The cops didn't come that night. They must have been eating a pizza or something. The break-and-enter person was being persistent, so eventually, I worked up the guts to leap out of bed, naked as a puppy, bashed on the inside of the door, and yelled in

Are You Thinking What I'm Thinking?
A Patchwork Journey Through My Life... So Far

my deepest, blokey voice, "FUCK OFF YOU THIEVING CUNTS, THE COPS ARE ON THEIR WAY!!" Quickly back to bed with the covers up, and the nervous little puppy had no more sleep that night. Dead-end street, huge oval, and big bushy park to escape through. Surely, the desperate junkies were coming to murder me! Apparently, they didn't, unless I went to another place and my life has been a dream since? It's possible.

Trumper Oval, Paddington

VW Golf Gti 2006

My current car. Who knows? It could be the last one I ever own? That's fine with me. Traded the Triton in. Why? Because I did a Masters Degree in teaching at Monash and didn't want to be on the tools for money anymore. Ladders, roofs, digging stump holes, crawling under sub floors just didn't appeal. So I drove to schools. Finished up doing some casual teaching which was quite enough for me. OMG I love this car with its sunroof, zoomy 2ltr turbo engine, 10 speaker sound system. Living in Elwood I cruise down to North Road boat launch area, open a traveller, eat peanuts, listen to music, trawl, then regret trawling fucking social media, watch sunsets... observe the world go by, smell the air, feel the atmosphere. Just sit by myself. Sit in the car. I like it. I'll do it until I die, I guess. A life-long car sitter. 'He made a small difference in the world and sat in his car.'... could be worse...

The Golf...

Wish Fairies, my favourite Banana special

When the starlight foundation came to the studio

These brave, beautiful kids were given this wish they had of meeting the Bananas and Teddies. Oh it was the most moving and wonderful thing to be able to do. Give these extraordinary humans this small but significant moment of joy. Oh my goodness, it is the least we can do. I needed recovery time after – I have kids. There but for the grace of luck and fate go we. We also went to a hospital to visit very sick kids. I think it was Royal Prince Alfred in Sydney. That was tricky! The fruit are 7'6" tall. Hospital ceilings are quite low. We had the brilliant costume department always with us to hold our hands and guide us –

we were pretty much blind in there. Down and around the halls and past the wards we went, bouncing and being jolly Bananas as best we could. There were lines of doctors and nursing staff applauding us as we went... my God, they are hero's on a daily basis. Finally we were taken so carefully into a ward with the sickest of kids, tubes and leads and machinery all around that we could not see. Heaven help us if we accidently pull out a tube! There were kids that had not smiled for six months laughing and crying with their parents and staff. What a gift for us to be able to do this small thing for these precious people.

Wowing the fans with large gesture and fruit-style slapstick.

(thank you, Greg Noakes, for the pic)

The Atrium

Some moments are so incredibly special as they're unfolding that you just want to cling to every single detail – the feeling, the memory, the smell, the temperature – everything, forever. So it can be recalled, and the true atmosphere of the occasion conjured up, making it feel just as fresh, real, and magnificent as it was in that very instant.

Here's one such moment...

It was a scorching hot January afternoon in 1993, right in the atrium area of the Sydney Opera House. My heavily pregnant partner, Rita,

Are You Thinking What I'm Thinking? A Patchwork Journey Through My Life... So Far

was setting up to play with her cool and groovy Jazz outfit, 'The Umbrellas'. Her oboe, a lovely old instrument notoriously susceptible to changes in temperature and humidity, was sitting in the direct sun. I could see the slight flicker of concern on her face about the intense heat, which seemed to envelop the entire band as they waited to perform.

The Oboe... with impossible double reed

She meticulously crafted her own reeds – specific lengths of bamboo, carefully cut, bent, and shaped. They were then folded in half over a piece of metal, achieving that final, perfect curvature, before being wrapped and tied with strong twine – sometimes red, sometimes green. The tie-off method at the end was unique to her. A small, sharp, chisel-like tool was her instrument for the delicate scraping and shaping. She'd keep several reeds on the go at all times, soaking them in mugs of water: the nice old one, a stand-by that would do just fine if the old one snapped, and a few others that were coming along nicely, needing to be 'played in' and worked up precisely to her liking.

The sun was absolutely belting through the huge windows. I could see her subtly shifting her instrument on its stand into the shade, a mug of water close by, and the reed case with her stand-bys at the ready.

Our baby was due in a week, perhaps two – our very first one. If it was a boy, he'd be Lyon; if a girl, Georgia. Rita was 'cooking' in the heat, as were the entire band: quirky, nerdy Peter on keys; James, the brilliant trombonist with those fabulous eyebrows that just wouldn't

Are You Thinking What I'm Thinking?
A Patchwork Journey Through My Life… So Far

quit; tall Steve on bass, a well-respected, fine player, Tim Hopkins, the good-looking young sax player brimming with potential; and Toby, a lovely man and a great jazz drummer.

They were working their way through the first set beautifully. The band had such a quiet sophistication about it, and the soloists were delightfully musical and irreverent all at once. The oboe was a relatively new addition. It's an instrument not often found in jazz ensembles. Rita was classically trained, having received Honours at the Rotterdam Conservatory. She'd played in shows, opera orchestras, and was a stand-by for the Sydney Symphony… now, she'd moved, taking a bold step towards that wonderful beast… Jazz!

But the sun was blazing. Her true test for today was coming: Erik Satie's *Gymnopédies* – the lovely, slow one. She'd told me it had taken her six years to finally 'get' her sound, and it was rich, free and beautiful. No wonder it took six years – have you ever tried to push air through that ridiculous little double reed? It's not surprising so many oboists develop physical problems.

I recall seeing her renowned tutor, Thomas Indermühle, at the Opera House as a guest of the Sydney Symphony Orchestra. When he played his first few notes, I shed tears of pride – "That's where she got it!" He was brilliant, and she was a chip off his block. She was a consummate professional, an absolute delight to watch and listen to…

But the sun was blazing…

So the tune started… it's beautifully composed… just piano – very simple – four bars, and here came her part… And just as her masterful tutor had gently but decisively swung his instrument out to confidently speak to his audience in the concert hall of this amazing building – so too did his brilliant student, Rita, gently swing that delightful old instrument out to speak to her audience, in the heat of the atrium – and the warm, pure, note-perfect, comforting tone of the oboe washed over us – with a precisely weighted amount of vibrato at the end of each phrase.

Are You Thinking What I'm Thinking? A Patchwork Journey Through My Life... So Far

Her hair was cut short, and she was wearing a loose, floral shirt with big, generous red and yellow flowers on it. Then, with the whole band respectfully watching, she gently moved and expertly encouraged that instrument to steadily find and hold the low octave note that other oboists wouldn't attempt – especially in that heat – and oh, she nailed it. The room was filled with the broad, comforting feeling that a low, generous oboe can give us. The band were all looking on and smiling as she confidently claimed that moment; then, as the true, disciplined professional she was, she stepped back to allow the next soloist – dear James – to come forward and wow us with his skill and playfulness, eyebrows twitching...

The set continued, and the band was enthusiastically applauded at the end. There were three distinct types of warmth in that room on that day. The fabulous and biting warmth of the January Sydney sun shining through glass... The warmth you can get from a group of highly trained jazz musos at the top of their game... And the warmth of pride you feel for someone very special to you doing a wonderful job when it's their time.

Baby Georgia was born two weeks later.

The Atrium overlooking the harbour... amazing location.

Are You Thinking What I'm Thinking?
A Patchwork Journey Through My Life... So Far

Bananas; some of the journey

I once filmed an educational/training film, about thirty minutes long, for the ABC. It was called "Voting", and its purpose was to teach secondary kids, probably Year 7 or 8, about the process of becoming a Member of Parliament. It featured some 'infotaining' content around how to form a political party, registering to vote, and all that. A really clever idea. In this comic-learning set-up, the 'lower' status character holds all the power and the vital information for the kids. The blustering protagonist, in turn, learns a few things and is put on the right path by the serf, or the fool, as is traditional. In this case, it's the cleaner. A tried-and-true storytelling device that has worked for hundreds, probably thousands, of years. "Voting" was penned by the fabulous Morris Gleitzman, a hugely successful children's writer. This would have been around 1990.

I played Genghis Khan, who makes his grand entrance in a puff of purple smoke late at night in the old Parliament House in Canberra. Full costumery: a big black top-knot wig, a fluffy jacket, furry animal-skin boots, a massive sword, and a big, gruff, confident voice. He's there, proclaiming ownership of the country with grand gestures and sword-waving, when we (the audience) suddenly spot the cleaner. He was played by the excellent Donato Caretti, who was actually in third year at NIDA when I was in first. The cleaner is casually vacuuming the floor when Genghis informs him that the country "is now mine!!" We actually shot it right there in the old Parliament House itself. I've got photos somewhere of me as Genghis, in full costume, reclining in the grand Speaker's chair, right there in the actual stately chamber in the Australian House of Parliament. Such a blast!

The cleaner, unfazed, simply says, "No, Mr Khan! You can't do it like that. Come with me, I'll show you how it's done!" And so, they embark on an adventure of discovery for dear old Genghis. Flying over the outback, looking at how the states are divided into wards, stumbling through the procedures and legislated requirements of running for Parliament. It's a steep learning curve for Genghis, but the cleaner is

Are You Thinking What I'm Thinking? A Patchwork Journey Through My Life... So Far

remarkably persuasive. And when he suddenly imagines Genghis as the lead singer for his grungy rock band? The whole thing culminates in a powerful, stadium rock song – which, get this, was written by Todd Hunter from Dragon! I even recorded the vocal in his home studio in Bondi Junction... so Sydney, so rock 'n' roll, such fun!

So there I was, on the steps of Parliament, waving a sword and belting out, "It would be much cheaper! Being an elected Rep. I could burn, I could pillage on these steps... AAAGGGGHHHHHH...." The gorgeous Maureen Green was in the band too, on keys. Another NIDA chum of mine!

A beautiful human and an excellent actor.

Maureen Green, Mr Khan and Danato Caretti. Voting, ABC

Are You Thinking What I'm Thinking?
A Patchwork Journey Through My Life… So Far

The steps of the old Parliament House, Canberra. Where Prime Minister Whitlam announce, 'Well may we say God save the Queen. Because nothing will save the Governor General.'… but today, Genghis had big plans.

This film was directed by Roger Bailey, an in-house director at the ABC known for his docos and bits of drama. I knew I'd get back to *Bananas* in this story, and sure enough, some months later, Roger got in touch with my agent at the time. He told her they were gearing up to shoot three, five-minute pilot episodes for a new live-action kids' show, based on the Carey Blyton tune, 'Bananas in Pyjamas'. This catchy little ditty had been sung by the great presenters of *Playschool* at the ABC for years. There were also those beloved stuffed toy Bananas that the likes of John Waters, Noni Hazlehurst, Philip Quast, John Hamblin, Benita Collings, George, Monica, and many more, played and danced with in that usual jolly, kid-friendly educational/fun style that made *Playschool* the best kids' show ever in this country – by a mile.

Roger wanted to know if I'd be interested in having a chat with him and the producer, Helena Harris, about playing one of the Bananas.

Are You Thinking What I'm Thinking? A Patchwork Journey Through My Life... So Far

Reluctantly, I went in to talk to them. I mean, seriously... did I do three years of classical training, currently doing some pretty decent work on feature films and interesting TV stuff, with my career sort of almost moving along okay... did I do all this to put on some bloody suit and bounce around? (Later, Nicholas and I would proudly claim we were 'classically trained Bananas'.)

So, I had the chat and said, "Okay, I'll do the three pilot episodes." There was no guarantee the thing would be greenlit, nobody would see my face anyway, it might be a bit of fun... and they were paying minimum ABC wages, so yeah, alright.

My recollection is that there was another meeting, a kind of read-through thing with Roger, Helena, and some bloke they were interested in to play the other Banana. Turns out it was Nicholas Opolski – I'd spent three years at NIDA with him and was absolutely thrilled when I heard his name! We kind of read through some stuff, mucked around with voices and moves and all that. Roger then asked, "Who wants to play B1?" "ME!" I enthused, possibly a little too exuberantly... and so it was. We agreed to do the three pilot episodes. This was the beginning of an amazing decade spent with this beautiful human, Mr Nicholas Opolski. OMG, how lucky was I that it was him. I honestly couldn't have endured the discomfort with another soul. He made it joyous, and together we were beautiful – a sort of clumsy, nongish beauty.

Are You Thinking What I'm Thinking?
A Patchwork Journey Through My Life... So Far

Described by one bloke as, a pair of Nongs!

I've said these things many times, and I'll keep saying them until I drop: Nicholas is one of life's true gentlemen. Working literally shoulder to shoulder with this man was an absolute gift in my life. He's funny, focused, passionate, dry, gentle, with a strong sense of social justice, and incredibly generous. He's one of the few people in my life who is genuinely 'okay with where he is' at any given moment; that is, he's endlessly curious about things. Even if it's not his usual 'bag', he'll ask questions and extend people the courtesy of his full attention.

Oh my goodness, the endless hours we spent together in rehearsal rooms, on set, in voice-over studios, travelling to and from places! Eating together, pondering the world, rigorously debating the text! They might have only been five-minute episodes, but we gave a damn, we gave a helluva damn! It mattered; it was work, and we respected it from top to bottom. There were times, both in the studio and in the voice-over rooms, when it felt like we were in some kind of perfect symmetry. We had fabulous, almost innate sync – and yet it was also

Are You Thinking What I'm Thinking? A Patchwork Journey Through My Life... So Far

delightfully, intentionally clunky. The 'fruit' (as they were often known) would almost always be in sheer panic, followed by a moment's silence, then an accepting, harmonious sigh, and a positive move forward, only to be challenged again by another seemingly insurmountable obstacle.

"Oh dear!"... "But wait! B2!!"... "Yes, B1?"... "Oh, sorry B2, I've forgotten."... "Never mind, B1, we'll just move these rocks, and everything will be alright."... "Oh, thanks, B2."... "You're welcome, B1..." (Trips over in a tall timber pratfall.) Together: "EEERRRGHH!"

The precision of the rehearsal, navigating sets and props whilst almost completely blind – so much of the work was done with a kind of 'body memory', like a goofy sort of dancing. We needed to have huge energy inside those suits, pumping out moves to bring the costumes to life and trying to add some sort of authentic 'Banana' type emotion to the moment. Classically trained Bananas indeed!

God, it was hot and uncomfortable, particularly in those prototype suits. Multiple layers of padding, foam, heavy costumes atop it all. And then the fibreglass heads! They were attached to a kind of bike helmet with prongs all around, fixed to the inside of these unwieldy heads, featuring a tiny slit of a mouth in a perpetual smile. This endless grin was covered in black mesh, and that was all of our vision once inside the suits. The entire weight of the fibreglass heads was, in fact, sitting directly on our heads. Not a lot of room for subtle movement. But we somehow made it work.

The actors playing the Teddies were Mary-Ann Henshaw, Jeremy Scrivener, and Sandy Lillingston – their characters named Amy, Morgan, and Lulu (after Helena's kids!). The Rat in a Hat was played by Shane McNamara. Wonderful folk, equally hard-working and inventive in their approach to the job. The green room was always lively. It was a great outfit. The fabulous Taylor Owynns played Lulu from series two to six. Eventually, we shot the pilot episodes. Then,

Are You Thinking What I'm Thinking?
A Patchwork Journey Through My Life… So Far

Bananas went away for a while as the post-production team wove their magic.

I was then confronted with a career choice: Do the thirty episodes of *Bananas* Series One, which had just been greenlit… or act in a small play that I'd been offered. Serious actor Kenneth, naturally, said yes to the play. This decision turned out to be an unfortunate one for me financially. I was paid a paltry $600 a week for the play, but as the classically trained Banana, I would have, over time, received tens of thousands of dollars in residuals for Series One of *Bananas*, which I had turned down! The first series went to video and sold upwards of 250,000 copies in Australia. A fabulous and happy success for all involved! The cast had a portion of the sales allotted to them as per Equity ruling. So, even though the daily shooting and rehearsal rate was really low, the back-end arrangement made it much better for the cast. Dear Duncan Wass, who replaced me as B1 in Series One, quite rightly received any residual payments for the work – and good on him!

The 'serious actor' play I chose to do was called Prin, produced by the Marian Street Theatre, situated in the leafy North Shore suburb of Killara. This thing was rehearsed and performed over six weeks in 1992, directed by Richard Cottrell. It featured Joan Sydney in the titular role, Elizabeth Alexander, Peter Whitford, Neil Fitzpatrick, myself, and Sancia Robinson. A pretty forgettable, Saturday afternoon matinee type of play that I remember very little about. Mostly, I recall looking out into the audience at a sea of blue rinse, grey hair, and the bright reflection of glasses.

So, I did the *Banana* pilot episodes, then Series 2, 3, 4, 5, and 6. Plus, maybe seven musical albums, four or five thirty-minute specials, and live appearances at ABC open days. We even performed at some theme park out west of Sydney for a week or two at one point. The show occupied us on and off for a ten-year period. I did plenty of other work during this time too – drove the cabs, sold the wine, dug the ditches, acted in movies and TV, had two beautiful kids, umpired a hundred footy games, hit the gym, made a couple of short films, developed screenplays, worked on corporate videos... The '90s, a pretty active time for young Kenneth in a multitude of ways.

A few more Banana notable moments:

Michael

It was a sad moment when we turned up for rehearsal one day; we saw several rock-and-roll roadie type chaps hanging around outside the studio. They were smoking, looking forlorn and slumped. INXS had booked the smaller studio for at least a couple of weeks to rehearse for their first tour in some time. This was the morning Michael Hutchence had been found deceased in his Double Bay hotel room. It was a profoundly sad time for fans and people in the entertainment industry. The gear remained set up in the studio for at least a week afterwards. I guess it had been paid for, and it would have been disrespectful and rather crass to dismantle it straight away. The whole situation felt very strange, of course. Rest in peace, Michael, and thank you, INXS, for the music.

The final hurrah...

We worked on the show for 10 years (I have an ABC plaque to prove it, and two gold records on the wall). I have no more memorabilia. Many moves and life changes mean that things get shed, lost, or left behind. However, I have lots of pictures and sweet memories of that rather amazing decade. I'm very thankful for the whole experience and very proud of what we achieved. It was a silly little show that could have easily just slid away after the three pilot episodes, but no! It didn't! Something like 230 episodes later, and so many other contributions. What a lucky fellow am I to be able to say I contributed significantly to this enduring cultural icon of Australian children's entertainment. Long live the fruit!

The show was discontinued in 2002. The ABC pulled down the sets and put the costumes into storage somewhere. We had a big party, of course. Then, a while later, the rights were sold to a company – I think it might have been Southern Star. They were planning to make an animated series of Bananas. They asked Nicholas and me if we would like to do the voices of the Bananas for the series. We chatted about this and decided against it. We felt like we had completed our work; we had been to the mountaintop. I think Nick might have been working on Neighbours at the time. Plus, as I recall, they were offering pretty crappy money – What's new? So, yeah – we let that one go.

The Russian Mafia and the Bananas

The head licensing person at the ABC during the fruit era was a terrific, entrepreneurial chap named Graeme Grasby. We hardly met him at the time. He was selling the show all over the world (something like 150 countries, I think) and was hugely responsible for the breadth of its reach. Recently, Nicholas, myself, and the wonderful Kerry O'Dowd Haretuku, who at that time was Head of Product Approval and Bananas Appearance Manager at ABC Children's, all met up. She was a fabulous support to us over the years – she actually walked the red carpet with us at the Logies in 1998. We got out of the limo looking fabulous in our suits. Kerry stepped out in the most glamorous gown; she is tall and striking with model-like good looks. She took our arms, and we all grinned our way up the red carpet, being snapped by the paparazzi in case we were famous! Kerry looked far more famous than us!

Anyway, Graeme recently invited us all to the Fred and Graeme chat in Melbourne at the toy fair. Fred is Fred Gaffney, who created heaps of Banana merchandise and did very well from it! Of course, we were never part of the merchandise aspect of Bananas; the suits are the famous ones; we were the brilliant operators inside them! Bringing the polystyrene to life! If our faces were poking through the heads, that would be a different story!

Graeme told a story we had never heard. This is my version of his story: as part of his job, he was travelling all over the world with some Banana suits to chat to TV networks, present the show, and sell, sell, sell. There are pictures of Bananas at the White House, the Tower of

Are You Thinking What I'm Thinking? A Patchwork Journey Through My Life... So Far

London, and various well-known landmarks. Graeme, on behalf of the ABC and indeed the people of Australia, wanted to introduce Bananas to Russia. The story goes that while he was there, the suits were stolen. Stolen! They were in sturdy road cases and well-protected for their world travels. He would just get some six-foot actor types to wear them for the photo opportunities. Nicholas and I could always tell they were frauds in the suits; no grace or subtlety at all.

In his hotel, Graeme received a call from someone with a Russian accent, apparently a colleague of the ABC licensing agent in Moscow. I mean, really? It's got to be the Russian mafia, doesn't it? This bloke was telling Graeme that "they" wanted $100,000 AUD for the return of the suits. Graeme got in touch with ABC Sydney, and the head honcho there told him there was no way the ABC would be bowing to blackmail and threats. "How much do the suits cost to make?" he asked. Graeme told him they cost $20,000 AUD to make. The ABC guy said, "Okay, maybe mention that figure to them, see what comes back." So, Graeme connected with this unknown person, mentioned the figure, and the guy said no, that wouldn't work, "they" want 100k. Graeme boarded a flight to London to carry on his great work of selling the show to the rest of the world, without the suits!

Nicholas and I couldn't help improvising what the Bananas are doing now in some dank, cold Russian gaol, awaiting rescue.

B1: I'm cold B2

B2: Me too B1

B1: Do you think they've forgotten about us B2?

B2: I don't think so B1. They're probably just very busy.

B1: Yes, very very busy B2.

B2: Another bowl of Borscht B1?

B1: Yes, that would be lovely B2

B2: (listening) But wait... Listen B1... what's that sound?

Are You Thinking What I'm Thinking?
A Patchwork Journey Through My Life… So Far

BREAKING NEWS!

The homecoming Kings. A special undercover QANTAS flight secreted our favourite fruit from Moscow to Cuddles Avenue direct! Thank you to ASIO, the SAS, the fast-talking Rat and the good people of Australia for freeing the Moscow 2! (or was it all a dream?)

A highlight I didn't expect; I recently did casual teaching; my last few months of working in the State education system in Victoria, mostly in outlying areas of greater Melbourne. A wonderful learning curve in many ways. Observing the distinct culture in each school, reflecting on why some appear healthier than others, student contentment, general respect, teaching staff satisfaction, equipment condition, school ground care, language use, mobile phone policies and the general 'vibe' of the schools. our education system is deeply unwell in many respects – I feel like I must write a little about this I keep working, and it's been a significant learning curve in many ways. I've observed the distinct cultures of each school, reflecting on why some appear healthier than others regarding student contentment, general respect, teaching staff satisfaction, equipment condition, school ground care, language use, phone policies, and overall engagement. Our education system, I've found, is deeply unwell in various aspects. I could easily launch into a tirade about why I believe this, but frankly, who cares? No one gives a damn what I think, and why should they?

Are You Thinking What I'm Thinking? A Patchwork Journey Through My Life... So Far

A small educational segue...

The hundreds of teachers I've interacted with over more than eight years are thoroughly dominated by the system we operate within. Principals and Headmasters, curriculum developers, leading teachers, learning experts, timetablers, aids – all of us are. From a structural, bureaucratic perspective, it's largely unfixable. This system, a monstrous entity metastasising since the industrial revolution, is now so vast and unwieldy that no government can, knows how to, or wants to change it. The results-oriented, standardised testing obsession driving our system stands in complete opposition to what educators in successful learning countries advocate. NAPLAN, for instance, was advised against by every university in the country during its planning stages. The ATAR is largely irrelevant in the real world. What we desperately need are flexible learning systems and, indeed, flexible, critically thinking, creative learners.

The question then becomes: how would the Finns approach this? Where does one even begin? At the bottom, that's where! I recall spending an afternoon listening to the eminent Finnish educator, author, and scholar Pasi Sahlberg during a Professional Development weekend with a couple of hundred secondary teachers. This was, in fact, the very professional development weekend I was driving to when I heard the Julia Louis-Dreyfus interview with Jane Fonda. Sahlberg was quite remarkable – a master of ironic PowerPoint data, a humble and inquisitive man possessing vast experience and knowledge without claiming to have all the answers. My kind of teacher, exactly. He concluded the session by suggesting that we, the teachers, need to initiate the education revolution that is needed. Governments simply cannot or will not. Instigating massive infrastructural change costs votes; people prefer the comfort of familiarity. Turning education and learning on its head would be an impossible task for them. Change began in Finland in 1949, a post-war shift echoing throughout Europe. Here, in this wide brown land, it's a daunting prospect.

Are You Thinking What I'm Thinking?
A Patchwork Journey Through My Life... So Far

So, we begin at the bottom. This means brave, creative principals in schools needing a fundamental shift – principals with a flexible vision and a team united in their direction. The change happens in the classroom, not at a government level. It's a slow, gradual process from the ground up. Look to the writings and TED Talks of the late, great English educator Ken Robinson; that's a starting point, alongside Mr Sahlberg's insights. That's where it all begins. The government might catch on over a decade or two, perhaps. Teaching is far too hard; it's no wonder people are abandoning the profession in droves across this country.

Anyways... back to Bananas...

So, there I was, casual teaching at various schools. Kids are always intrigued by a casual teacher who looks a bit different or has something about them that sparks their interest. I suppose I fit that description because, inevitably, they Google me. "Sir! Are you an actor?" The presence of even a small piece of celebrity excites them enormously – "The power of 'fame,' Sir!" "Were you in *Pirates of the Caribbean*?" "Did you work with Johnny Depp?"

"WAIT!!! Were you in *Bananas in Pyjamas*?" "OMG, Sir! You are my childhood!!!"

These kids are typically between 12 and 16 years old. They were born more than a decade after we finished shooting the show. I often ask them, "Wasn't I your parents' childhood?" It's astonishing. They watch both the 'live-action' Bananas and the animated series. Invariably, they say they prefer the suited Bananas. And honestly, who wouldn't? The point here is the enduring presence of Bananas as a solid, permanent fixture in the fabric of Australian culture. They're still incredibly popular. At the last school I worked at in mid-2024, I signed over 300 B1 autographs for students. I never refuse. If they want one, they get one. They queue up, so appreciative of this tiny gesture I can offer. "Of course!" I tell them. They ask me to do the voice. I make them help me: "You do the B2 part... Are you thinking what I'm thinking, B1?" (I insist they do it with the same crazy high energy we used to). "I think

Are You Thinking What I'm Thinking? A Patchwork Journey Through My Life... So Far

I am, B2." (Together...) "It's recess tiiiiiime!!!! Now get out!" I say. They laugh and run off with a bit of joy.

It's the very least I can do.

"Thank you for keeping the Banana flame burning," I often write for them.

B2 finally loses his shit!

We were being led on the rather long walk along a gravel path from the dressing rooms to the stage for our final live performance at a place called Australia's Wonderland, somewhere west of Sydney. It was a huge theme park with hundreds of rides and fun things for kids. We'd agreed to perform our 20-minute live show there for the ABC for a week or two – four or five shows a day. It was decent money, I got to be with my friend, and we enjoyed the passage of time. For the very last show, there we were, being guided by the wonderful costume department – they always held our hands to prevent us hurting a child, or indeed falling and soiling the costumes! I turned and noticed four or five boys, around ten years old I'd guess, walking a few metres behind us. I detected some snickering, just boys being boys... then suddenly, one of them threw a tennis ball full pelt, bouncing it off B2's head! Nicholas spun around and yelled at the top of his voice, "FUCK OFF, KID!" I nearly collapsed with laughter!

Are You Thinking What I'm Thinking?
A Patchwork Journey Through My Life... So Far

The Rat looks off into the future, Morgan wonders about the pink moon, Lulu busies herself with plans as Amy is mesmerised by the Bananas mime skills transporting her onto a big, big aeroplane to take us all far, far away...

Are You Thinking What I'm Thinking? A Patchwork Journey Through My Life... So Far

A Random Gallery...

Kenny Rogered, taking care of business with Stevie Blissbomb and Throbbing Glitterous from Glam Jam... the rock continues

The Rentman, my first film. With the delightful Hazel Townsend

Are You Thinking What I'm Thinking?
A Patchwork Journey Through My Life... So Far

Donald Radley searching for his wife Joyce – Regal Wheel Race 1954

Buried Child, with Kate Mulvaney, Belvoir St Theatre 2003

Are You Thinking What I'm Thinking? A Patchwork Journey Through My Life... So Far

The Rain Dancers, with the late Monica Maughan, Malthouse Theatre 2002

Inside 2000 with James Wardlaw, Malthouse Theatre 2000

Are You Thinking What I'm Thinking?
A Patchwork Journey Through My Life… So Far

Alan Glover, Joe vs Carole (Stan) 2022

Frankenstein, Yellow Pages commercial, late 1980s

Are You Thinking What I'm Thinking? A Patchwork Journey Through My Life... So Far

Some of the Fields of Fire team, 1986

Tonight, and Forever, Second year NIDA 1983

Are You Thinking What I'm Thinking?
A Patchwork Journey Through My Life… So Far

Miss Fisher's Murder Mysteries, season 3

Calling the agent? Circa 1975

Are You Thinking What I'm Thinking? A Patchwork Journey Through My Life… So Far

Babe 2

Force of Nature, The Dry 2   Fake, with the late, wonderful Janet Andrewartha - RIP

Are You Thinking What I'm Thinking?
A Patchwork Journey Through My Life… So Far

Successful completion of the deck

A chunked out E chord on a Saturday afternoon… rock and roll will never die!

Are You Thinking What I'm Thinking? A Patchwork Journey Through My Life… So Far

Outro

Hey dear reader,

If you stuck with this for the 60,000 words, I congratulate you! Here I'd like to acknowledge and thank some, but not all folks. I'm bound to leave someone out. It's ok, I'll get you later for a personal thanks!

Thank you everyone that has helped me along the road to where I am today, in all of the areas and in all of the ways. I know I'm lucky; incalculably lucky to even be alive, and to live this life. The whole thing makes me want to grab a traveller and some salty snacks, turn up some kick arse Oz rock, park down near the water on a warm afternoon and simply sit and reflect.

My forever love and deepest thanks to my family:

Georgia Radley

Angus Radley

Marvin Radley Bell

Angelica Bell Radley

Jane Williamson

John Radley

Peter Radley

Stuart Radley

Shane Radley

Are You Thinking What I'm Thinking?
A Patchwork Journey Through My Life… So Far

Acknowledgements

My friends and close connections – Big love and respect to all of these excellent people that have given me joy, love, learning, laughs, music, art, support and made a difference to my life; Greg Stone, Shayne Francis, Shane Connor, Nicholas Opolski, Robert Price, Tricia Radley, Rita van Ooi, Elizabeth Huntly, Ian Scott, James Roden, Gabi Rowland, David Haig Brown, the late Kenny Hughes, Fleur Peppard, Steve Haslam, James Dickson, Gary Dyson, Peter Semple, Mark Smith, Lindsay Hodgson, Sir Leslie Thornton, Tracey Haughton, Evan Clarry, Lachlan Ker, Steve Mouzakis, Teresa Bell, Peter Hurry, Raj Sidhu, Jeremy Stanford, Alex Morcos, Trevor Stewart, Jan Stroek, Rob Murdoch, Mark Ferrugia, Timothy Robinson, Morgan Kurrajong, Nara Dragsnes… and you, the person I accidently left out, big Radley style love to you too!

I would also like to the thank the team at Australian Book Publishers for their help in making this book a success.

Are You Thinking What I'm Thinking? A Patchwork Journey Through My Life… So Far

A personal encore: (what's the point if I don't?)

You know, I always kind of felt like I have a big heart. Like I have a lot of love. I always feel proud of people that try hard, that are a bit brave, that work through stuff, stand up for what's right, that forgive, accept, be quiet and generous. I always felt I had a decent helping of those kinds of qualities in me. Maybe folks feel that or read that in me somehow. I just want to say here that I wish love and reasonable satisfaction for the people I have been close to. In both big connections, I mean in love and family and relationships, and in the other connections like storytelling, work and study. And the smaller meeting places – and there have been so many... like my barista and my mechanic and the baker... I actually, from the bottom of my heart wish nice things for all of you people; family, friends, lovers, partners, work mates and collaborators... and the guy down the street on the bench that I talk to. I hope you're ok, the moments we had and have together are real and so valuable for me. Thank you.

I wish you peace.

This book is a beginning of course.

It's all beginnings.

See you on the next one.

From my heart,

Kenneth x

www.ingramcontent.com/pod-product-compliance
Lightning Source LLC
Chambersburg PA
CBHW020406080526
44584CB00014B/1190